Holland

and

Germany

Jacques Casanova de Seingalt

[ZHINGOORA BOOKS]

THE ETERNAL QUEST

HOLLAND AND GERMANY

CHAPTER X

Portrait of the Pretended Countess Piccolomini—Quarrel and Duel—Esther and Her Father, M. D'O.—Esther Still Taken with the Cabala—Piccolomini Forges a Bill of Exchange: Results I Am Fleeced, and in Danger of Being Assassinated—Debauch with the Two Paduan Girls—I Reveal A Great Secret

To Esther—I Bate the Rascally St. Germain; His Flight—Manon Baletti Proves Faithless to Me; Her Letter Announcing Her Marriage: My Despair—Esther Spends a Day With Me—My Portrait and My Letters to Manon Get Into Esther's Hands—I Pass a Day with Her—We Talk of Marrying Each Other

The so-called Countess Piccolomini was a fine example of the adventurers. She was young, tall, well-made, had eyes full of fire, and skin of a dazzling whiteness; not, however, that natural whiteness which delights those who know the value of a satin skin and rose petals, but rather that artificial fairness which is commonly to be seen at Rome on the faces of courtezans, and which disgusts those who know how it is produced. She had also splendid teeth, glorious hair as black as jet, and arched eyebrows like ebony. To these advantages she added attractive manners, and there was something intelligent about the way she spoke; but through all I saw the adventuress peeping out, which made me detest her.

As she did not speak anything but Italian the countess had to play the part of a mute at table, except where an English officer named Walpole was concerned, who, finding her to his taste, set himself to amuse her. I felt friendly disposed towards this Englishman, though my feelings were certainly not the result of sympathy. If I had been blind or deaf Sir James Walpole would have been totally indifferent to me, as what I felt for him was the result of my observation.

Although I did not care for the countess, for all that I went up to her room after dinner with the greater part of the guests. The count arranged a game of whist, and Walpole played at primero with the countess, who cheated him in a masterly manner; but though he saw it he laughed and paid, because it suited his purpose to do so. When he had lost fifty Louis he called quarter, and the countess asked him to take her to the theatre. This was what the good-natured Englishman wanted; and he and the countess went off, leaving the husband playing whist.

I, too, went to the play, and as chance would have it my neighbour in the pit was Count Tot, brother to the count famous for his stay in Constantinople.

We had some conversation together, and he told me he had been obliged to leave France on account of a duel which he had had with a man who had jested with him for not being present at the battle of Minden, saying that he had absented himself in view of the battle. The count had proved his courage with the sword on the other's body—a rough kind of argument which was fashionable then as now. He told me he had no money, and I immediately put my purse at his service; but, as the saying goes, a kindness is never thrown away, and five years later he did the same by me at St. Petersburg. Between the acts he happened to notice the Countess Piccolomini, and asked me if I knew her husband. "I know him very slightly," I answered, "but we happen to be staying at the same hotel."

"He's a regular black sheep," said the count, "and his wife's no better than he."

It seemed that they had already won a reputation in the town.

After the play I went back to the hotel by myself, and the head-waiter told me that Piccolomini had set out hot-foot with his servant, his only luggage being a light portmanteau. He did not know the reason of this sudden departure, but a minute afterwards the countess came in, and her maid having whispered something to her she told me that the count had gone away because he had fought a duel but that often happened. She asked me to sup with her and Walpole, and her appetite did not seem to suffer from the absence of her spouse.

Just as we were finishing supper, an Englishman, who had been of the whist party, came up and told Walpole that the Italian had been caught cheating and had given the lie to their fellow Englishman, who had detected him, and that they had gone out together. An hour afterwards the Englishman returned with two wounds, one on the fore-arm and one on the shoulder. It was a trifling affair altogether.

Next day, after I had had dinner with the Comte d'Afri, I found a letter from Piccolomini, with an enclosure addressed to the countess, waiting for me at the inn. He begged me to give his wife the letter, which would inform her of his plans, and then to bring her to the Ville de Lyon at Amsterdam, where he was staying. He wanted to know how the Englishman whom he had wounded was getting on.

The duty struck me as an amusing one, and I should have laughed with all my heart if I had felt the least desire to profit by the confidence he was pleased to place in me. Nevertheless I went up to the countess, whom I found sitting up in bed playing with Walpole. She read the letter, told me that she could not start till the day following, and informed me what time she would go, as if it had been all settled; but I smiled sardonically, and told her that my business kept me at the Hague, and that I could not possibly escort her. When Walpole heard me say this he offered to be my substitute, to which she agreed. They set out the day following, intending to lie at Leyden.

Two days after their departure, I was sitting down to dinner with the usual company, increased by two Frenchmen who had just come. After the soup one of them said, coolly,

"The famous Casanova is now in Holland."

"Is he?" said the other, "I shall be glad to see him, and ask for an explanation which he will not like."

I looked at the man, and feeling certain that I had never seen him before

I began to get enraged; but I merely asked the fellow if he knew Casanova.

"I'll ought to know him," said he, in that self-satisfied tone which is always so unpleasant.

"Nay, sir, you are mistaken; I am Casanova."

Without losing his self-possession, he replied, insolently,

"You are really very much mistaken if you think you are the only Casanova in the world."

It was a sharp answer, and put me in the wrong. I bit my lips and held my tongue, but I was grievously offended, and determined to make him find the Casanova who was in Holland, and from whom he was going to extract an unpleasant explanation, in myself. In the meanwhile I bore as well as I could the poor figure he must be cutting before the officers at table, who, after hearing the insolence of this young blockhead, might take me for a coward. He, the insolent fellow, had no scruple in abusing the triumph his answer had given him, and talked away in the random fashion. At last he forgot himself so far as to ask from what country I came.

"I am a Venetian, sir," I replied.

"Ah! then you are a good friend to France, as your republic is under
French protection."

At these words my ill-temper boiled over, and, in the tone of voice one uses to put down a puppy, I replied that the Republic of Venice was strong enough to do without the protection of France or of any other power, and that during the thirteen centuries of its existence it had had many friends and allies but no protectors. "Perhaps," I ended, "you will reply by begging my pardon for not knowing that these was only one Venice in the world."

I had no sooner said this than a burst of laughter from the whole table set me right again. The young blockhead seemed taken aback and in his turn bit his lips, but his evil genius made him, strike in again at dessert. As usual the conversation went from one subject to another, and we began to talk about the Duke of Albermarle. The Englishmen spoke in his favour, and said that if he had been alive there would have been no war between England and France; they were probably right, but even if the duke had lived war might have broken out, as the two nations in question have never yet succeeded in understanding that it is for both their interests to live at peace together. Another Englishman praised Lolotte, his mistress. I said I had seen that charming woman at the Duchess of Fulvi's, and that no one deserved better to become the Countess of Eronville. The Count of Eronville, a lieutenant-general and a man of letters, had just married her.

I had scarcely finished what I had to say when Master Blockhead said, with a laugh, that he knew Lolotte to be a good sort of girl, as he had slept with her at Paris. I could restrain myself no longer; my indignation and rage consumed me. I took up my plate, and made as if I would throw it at his head, saying at the same time,

"You infernal liar!" He got up, and stood with his back to the fire, but I could see by his sword-knot that he was a soldier.

Everybody pretended not to hear anything of this, and the conversation went on for some time on indifferent subjects; and at last they all rose from their seats and left the room.

My enemy said to his companion that they would see one another again after the play, and remained by the fire, with his elbow resting on the chimney-piece. I remained at table till the company had all left the room, and when we were alone together I got up and looked him straight in the face, and went out, walking towards Sheveningue, sure that he would follow me if he were a man of any mettle. When I had got to some distance from the hotel I looked round, and saw that he was following me at a distance of fifty paces.

When I got to the wood I stopped at a suitable place, and stood awaiting my antagonist. He was ten paces off when he drew his sword, and I had plenty of time to draw mine though he came on fast. The fight did not last long, for as soon as he was near enough I gave him a thrust which has never failed me, and sent him back quicker than he came. He was wounded in the chest above the right breast, but as my sword was flat and the opening large enough the wound bled easily. I lowered my sword and ran up to him, but I could do nothing; he said that we should meet again at Amsterdam, if I was going there, and that he would have his revenge. I saw him again five or six years afterwards at Warsaw, and then I did him a kindness. I heard afterwards that his name was Varnier, but I do not know whether he was identical with the president of the National Convention under the infamous Robespierre.

I did not return to the hotel till after the play, and I then heard that the Frenchman, after having the surgeon with him for an hour, had set out for Rotterdam with his friend. We had a pleasant supper and talked cheerfully together without a word being said about the duel, with the exception that an English lady said, I forget in what connection, that a man of honour should never risk sitting down to dinner at an hotel unless he felt inclined, if necessary, to fight. The remark was very true at that time, when one had to draw the sword for an idle word, and to expose one's self to the consequences of a duel, or else be pointed at, even by the ladies, with the finger of scorn.

I had nothing more to keep me at the Hague, and I set out next morning before day-break for Amsterdam. On the way I stopped for dinner and recognized Sir James Walpole, who told me that he had started from Amsterdam the evening before, an hour after giving the countess into her husband's charge. He said that he had got very tired of her, as he had nothing more to get from a woman who gave more than one asked, if one's purse-strings were opened wide enough. I got to Amsterdam about midnight and took up my abode at "The Old Bible." The neighbourhood of Esther had awakened my love for that charming girl, and I was so impatient to see her that I could not sleep.

I went out about ten o'clock and called on M. d'O, who welcomed me in the friendliest manner and reproached me for not having alighted at his house. When he heard that I had given up business he congratulated me on not having removed it into Holland, as I should have been ruined. I did not tell him that I had nearly come to that in France, as I considered such a piece of information would not assist my designs. He complained bitterly of the bad faith of the French Government, which had involved him in considerable losses; and then he asked me to come and see Esther.

I was too impatient to embrace her to stay to be asked twice; I ran to greet her. As soon as she saw me she gave a cry of surprise and delight, and threw herself in my arms, where I received her with fondness equal to her own. I found her grown and improved; she looked lovely. We had scarcely sat down when she told me that she had become as skilled in the cabala as myself.

"It makes my life happy," said she, "for it gives me a power over my father, and assures me that he will never marry me to anyone but the man of my choice."

"I am delighted that you extract the only good that can proceed from this idle science, namely, the power to guide persons devoid of strength of will. But your father must think that I taught you the secret?"

"Yes, he does; and he said, one day, that he would forgive me any sacrifices I might have made to obtain this precious secret from you."

"He goes a little further than we did, my dearest Esther."

"Yes, and I told him that I had gained it from you without any sacrifice, and that now I was a true Pythoness without having to endure the torments of the tripod; and I am sure that the replies you gave were invented by yourself."

"But if that were so how could I have known where the pocket-book was, or whether the ship was safe?"

"You saw the portfolio yourself and threw it where it was discovered, and as for the vessel you spoke at random; but as you are an honest man, confess that you were afraid of the results. I am never so bold as that, and when my father asks me questions of that kind, my replies are more obscure than a sibyl's. I don't wish him to lose confidence in my oracle, nor do I wish him to be able to reproach me with a loss that would injure my own interests."

"If your mistake makes you happy I shall leave you in it. You are really a woman of extraordinary talents—, you are quite unique."

"I don't want your compliments," said she, in a rather vexed manner, "I want a sincere avowal of the truth."

"I don't think I can go as far as that."

At these words, which I pronounced in a serious way, Esther went into a reverie, but I was not going to lose the superiority I had over her, and racked my brains to find some convincing prediction the oracle might make to her, and while I was doing so dinner was announced.

There were four of us at table, and I concluded that the fourth of the party must be in love with Esther, as he kept his eyes on her the whole time. He was her father's favourite clerk, and no doubt her father would have been glad if she had fallen in love with him, but I soon saw that she was not likely to do so. Esther was silent all through dinner, and we did not mention the cabala till the clerk was gone.

"Is it possible," said M. d'O, "for my daughter to obtain the answers of the oracle without your having taught her?"

"I always thought such a thing impossible till to-day," I answered, "but Esther has convinced me that I was mistaken. I can teach the secret to no one without losing it myself, for the oath I swore to the sage who taught me forbids me to impart it to another under pain of forfeiture. But as your daughter has taken no such oath, having acquired it herself, she may be for all I know at perfect liberty to communicate the secret to anyone."

Esther, who was as keen as a razor, took care to say that the same oath that I had taken had been imposed on her by the oracle, and that she could not communicate the cabalistic secret to anyone without the permission of her genius, under pain of losing it herself.

I read her inmost thoughts, and was rejoiced to see that her mind was calmed. She had reason to be grateful to me, whether I had lied or not, for I had given her a power over her father which a father's kindness could not have assured; but she perceived that what I had said about her oracular abilities had been dictated merely by politeness, and she waited till we were alone to make me confess as much.

Her worthy father, who believed entirely in the infallibility of our oracles, had the curiosity to put the same question to both of us, to see if we should agree in the answer. Esther was delighted with the idea, as she suspected that the one answer would flatly contradict the other, and M. d'O having written his question on two sheets of paper gave them to us. Esther went up to her own room for the operation, and I questioned the oracle on the table at which we had had dinner, in the presence of the father. Esther was quick, as she came down before I had extracted from the pyramid the letters which were to compose my reply, but as I knew what to say as soon as I saw her father read the answer she gave him I was not long in finishing what I had to do.

M. d'O—— asked if he should try to get rid of the French securities he held in spite of the loss he would incur by selling out.

Esther's oracle replied,

"You must sow plentifully before you reap. Pluck not up the vine before the season of the vintage, for your vine is planted in a fruitful soil."

Mine ran as follows:—

"If you sell out you will repent, for there will be a new comptroller-general, who will pay all claims before another year has elapsed."

Esther's answer was conceived in the sibylline style, and I admired the readiness of her wit; but mine went right to the point, and the worthy man embraced us joyfully, and, taking his hat and stick, said that since our replies agreed he would run the risk of losing three million francs and make a profit of five or six hundred thousand in the course of the year. His daughter began to recant, and would have warned him against the danger, but he, who was as firm as a Mussulman, kissed her again, saying,

"The oracle is not wont to lie, and even if it does deceive me this time it will only be a fourth part of my fortune that I shall lose."

When Esther and I were alone I began to compliment her, much to her delight, on the cleverness of her answer, the elegance of her style, and her boldness, for she could not be as well acquainted with French affairs as I was.

"I am much obliged to you," said she, "for having confirmed my reply, but confess that you lied to please me."

"I confess, since that will please you, and I will even tell you that you have nothing more to learn."

"You are a cruel man! But how could you reply that there would be another comptroller-general in a year's time, and run the risk of compromising the oracle? I never dare to say things like that; I love the oracle too well to expose it to shame and confusion."

"That shews that I do not invent the answers; but since the oracle has pronounced it I am willing to bet that Silhouette will be dismissed."

"Your obstinacy drives me to despair, for I shall not rest till I know that I am as much a master of the cabala as you are, and yet you will not confess that you invent the answers yourself. For charity's sake do something to convince me of the contrary."

"I will think it over."

I passed the whole day with this delightful girl, whose amiable disposition and great wealth would have made me a happy man if it were not for my master-passion, the love of independence, and my aversion to make up my mind to live for the rest of my days in Holland.

In the course of my life I have often observed that the happiest hours are often the heralds of misfortune. The very next day my evil genius took me to the Ville de Lyon. This was the inn where Piccolomini and his wife were staying, and I found them there in the midst of a horde of cheats and sharpers, like themselves. As soon as the good people heard my name they rushed forward, some to greet me, and others to have a closer look at me, as if I were some strange wild beast. Amongst those present were a Chevalier de Sabi, who wore the uniform of a Polish major, and protested he had known me at Dresden; a Baron de Wiedan, claiming Bohemia as his fatherland, who greeted me by saying that his friend the Comte St. Germain had arrived at the Etoile d'Orient, and had been enquiring after me; an attenuated-looking bravo who was introduced to me as the Chevalier de la Perine, whom I recognized at the first glance as the fellow called Talvis, who had robbed the Prince-Bishop of Presburg, who had lent me a hundred Louis the same day, and with whom I had fought a duel at Paris. Finally, there was an Italian named Neri, who looked like a blacksmith minus his honesty, and said that he remembered seeing me one evening at the casino. I recollected having seen him at the place where I met the wretched Lucie.

In the midst of this band of cut-purses I saw the so-called wife of the pretended Chevalier de Sabi, a pretty woman from Saxony, who, speaking Italian indifferently well, was paying her addresses to the Countess Piccolomini.

I bit my lips with anger to find myself in such honourable company, but putting a good face on a bad game I greeted everybody politely, and then drawing a roll of a hundred Louis from my pocket I presented them to Master Perine Talvis, telling him I was glad to be able to return them to him with my best thanks.

My politeness did not meet with much of a reception, for the impudent scoundrel answered me, as he pocketed the money, that he remembered having lent it me at Presburg, but he also remembered a more important matter.

"And pray what is that?" said I, in a dry and half-disdainful tone.

"You owe me a revenge at the sword's point, as you know right well. Here is the mark of the gash you gave me seven years ago."

So saying, the wretched little man opened his shirt and shewed the small round scar. This scene, which belonged more to farce than comedy, seemed to have struck all tongues with paralysis.

"Anywhere else than in Holland, where important and delicate business debars me from fighting, I shall be glad to meet you and mark you again, if you still desire to cross swords with me; but while I am here I must beg you not to disturb me. All the same, you may as well know that I never go out without a couple of friends in my pockets, and that if you attack me I shall blow your brains out in self-defence."

"My revenge must be with crossed swords," said he. "However, I will let you finish your business."

"You will do wisely."

Piccolomini, who had been casting a hungry eye upon my hundred louis, proposed immediately afterwards a bank at faro, and began to deal. Prudence would have restrained me from playing in such company, but the dictates of prudence were overcome by my desire to get back the hundred louis which I had given Talvis, so I cut in. I had a run of bad luck and lost a hundred ducats, but, as usual, my loss only excited me. I wished to regain what I had lost, so I stayed to supper, and afterwards, with better luck, won back my money. I was content to stop at this, and to let the money I had paid to Talvis go, so I asked Piccolomini to pay me, which he did with a bill of exchange on an Amsterdam bank drawn by a firm in Middlesburg. At first I made some difficulty in taking it, on the pretext that it would be difficult to negotiate, but he promised to let me have the money next day, and I had to give in.

I made haste to leave this cut-throat place, after refusing to lend Talvis a hundred Louis, which he wanted to borrow of me on the strength of the revenge I owed him. He was in a bad humour, both on this account and because he had lost the hundred Louis I had paid him, and he allowed himself to use abusive language, which I treated with contempt. I went to bed, promising myself never to set foot in such a place again.

The next morning, however, I went out with the intention of calling on Piccolomini to get the bill of exchange cashed, but on my way I happened to go into a coffee-house and to meet Rigerboos, Therese's friend, whose acquaintance the reader has already made. After greeting each other, and talking about Therese, who was now in London and doing well, I skewed him my bill, telling him the circumstances under which I had it. He looked at it closely, and said,

"It's a forgery, and the original from which it was copied was honoured yesterday."

He saw that I could scarcely believe it, and told me to come with him to be convinced of the truth of what he said.

He took me to a merchant of his acquaintance, who skewed me the genuine bill, which he had cashed the day before for an individual who was unknown to him. In my indignation I begged Rigerboos to come with me to Piccolomini, telling him that he might cash it without remark, and that otherwise he would witness what happened.

We arrived at the count's and were politely received, the count asking me to give him the bill and he would send it to the bank to be cashed, but Rigerboos broke in by saying that it would be dishonoured, as it was a mere copy of a bill which had been cashed the evening before.

Piccolomini pretended to be greatly astonished, and said that, "though he could not believe it, he would look into the matter."

"You may look into it when you please," said I, "but in the mean time I should be obliged by your giving me five hundred florins."

"You know me, sir," said he, raising his voice, "I guarantee to pay you, and that ought to be enough."

"No doubt it would be enough, if I chose; but I want my money."

At this his wife came in and began to take her part in the dispute, and on the arrival of the count's man, a very cut-threat, Rigerboos took hold of me by the arm and drew me forcibly away. "Follow me," said he, when we were outside, "and let me see to this business myself." He took me to a fine-looking man, who turned out to be the lieutenant of police, and after he had heard the case he told me to give him the bill of exchange and to say where I was going to dine. I told him I should be at M. d'O 's, and saying that would do he went off. I thanked Rigerboos, and went to Esther, who reproached me tenderly for not having been to see her the evening before. That flattered me, and I thought her a really charming girl.

"I must take care," said I, "not to see you every day, for your eyes have a sway over me that I shall not be able to resist much longer."

"I shall believe as much of that as I choose, but, by-the-by, have you thought of any way of convincing me?"

"What do you want to be convinced about?"

"If it be true that there is in your cabala an intelligence distinct from your own you ought to be able to find some way of proving it to me."

"That is a happy thought; I will think it over."

At that moment her father came in from the Exchange, and we sat down to dinner.

We were at dessert when a police official brought me five hundred florins, for which I gave him a receipt.

When he had gone I told my entertainers what had happened the evening before and in the morning, and the fair Esther reproached me for preferring such bad company to her. "By way of punishment," said she, "I hope you will come with me to the theatre this evening, though they are going to give a Dutch play, of which you will not understand a word."

"I shall be near you, and that is enough for me."

In fact, I did not comprehend a word of the actors' gibberish, and was terribly bored, as Esther preserved a solemn and serious silence the whole time.

As we were coming from the theatre she told me all about the piece with charming grace and wonderful memory; she seemed to wish to give me some pleasure in return for the tedium to which she had condemned me. When we got home we had supper, and that evening, Heaven be thanked! I heard nothing more about the cabala. Before we parted, Esther and her father made me promise to dine with them every day, and to let them know if anything prevented my coming.

Next morning, about eight o'clock, while I was still dressing, I suddenly saw Piccolomini standing before me, and as he had not sent in his name I began to feel suspicious. I rang the bell for my faithful Spaniard, who came in directly.

"I want to speak to you privately," said he, "tell that fellow to go out."

"He can stay," I answered, "he does not know a word of Italian." Le Duc, of course, knew Italian perfectly well.

"Yesterday, about noon," he began, "two men came into my room. They were accompanied by the innkeeper, who served as interpreter. One of the men asked me if I felt inclined to cash there and then a forged bill of exchange, which I had given the night before, and which he held in his hands. As I gave no reply, he told me that there was no time for consideration or argument; I must say yes or no there and then, for such were their instructions from the chief of police. I had no choice in the matter, so I paid the five hundred florins, but I did not get back the bill, and the man told me I could not have it unless I told the police the name of the person from whom I got it, as, in the interests of commerce, the forger must be prosecuted. My reply was that I could not possibly tell them what they wanted, as I had got it of a stranger who had come into my room while I was holding a small bank of faro, to pass the time.

"I told him that after this person (who I had thought introduced by someone in the company) had gone, I found to my surprise that nobody knew him; and I added that if I had been aware of this I would not only have refused the bill but would not have allowed him to play. Thereupon the second policeman said that I had better find out who this person was, or else I should be considered as the forger and prosecuted accordingly; after this threat they went out.

"In the afternoon my wife called on the chief of police and was politely received, but after hearing what she had to say he informed her that she must find out the forger, since M. Casanova's honour might be endangered by the banker taking proceedings against him, in which case he would have to prosecute me.

"You see in what a difficult position we are placed, and I think you ought to try to help us. You have got your money and you are not without friends. Get their influence exerted in the matter, and we shall hear no more about it. Your interests as well as mine are concerned."

"Except as a witness of the fact," I answered, "I can have nothing to do with this affair. You agree that I received the bill from you, since you cashed it; that is enough for me. I should be glad to be of service to you, but I really don't see what I can do. The best advice I can give you is to make a sacrifice of the rascally sharper who gave you the forged bill, and if you can't do that I would counsel you to disappear, and the sooner the better, or else you may come to the galleys, or worse."

He got into a rage at this, and turning his back on me went out, saying I should be sorry for what I had said.

My Spaniard followed him down the stair and came back to tell me that the signor had gone off threatening vengeance, and that, in his opinion, I would do well to be on my guard.

"All right," said I, "say no more about it."

All the same I was really very grateful for his advice, and I gave the matter a good deal of thought.

I dressed myself and went to see Esther, whom I had to convince of the divinity of my oracle, a different task with one whose own wits had told her so much concerning my methods. This was the problem she gave me to solve,

"Your oracle must tell me something which I, and only I, know."

Feeling that it would be impossible to fulfil these conditions, I told her that the oracle might reveal some secret she might not care to have disclosed.

"That is impossible," she answered, "as the secret will be known only to myself."

"But, if the oracle replies I shall know the answer as well as you, and it may be something you would not like me to know."

"There is no such thing, and, even if there were, if the oracle is not your own brain you can always find out anything you want to know."

"But there is some limit to the powers of the oracle."

"You are making idle excuses; either prove that I am mistaken in my ideas or acknowledge that my oracle is as good as yours."

This was pushing me hard, and I was on the point of declaring myself conquered when a bright idea struck me.

In the midst of the dimple which added such a charm to her chin Esther had a little dark mole, garnished with three or four extremely fine hairs. These moles, which we call in Italian 'neo, nei', and which are usually an improvement to the prettiest face, when they occur on the face, the neck, the arms, or the hands, are duplicated on the corresponding parts of the body. I concluded, therefore, that Esther had a mole like that on her chin in a certain place which a virtuous girl does not shew; and innocent as she was I suspected that she herself did not know of this second mole's existence. "I shall astonish her," I said to myself, "and establish my superiority in a manner which will put the idea of having equal skill to mine out of her head for good." Then with the solemn and far-away look of a seer I made my pyramid and extracted these words from it,

"Fair and discreet Esther, no one knows that at the entrance of the temple of love you have a mole precisely like that which appears on your chin."

While I was working at my calculations, Esther was leaning over me and following every movement. As she really knew as much about the cabala as I did she did not want it to be explained to her, but translated the numbers into letters as I wrote them down. As soon as I had extracted all the combinations of numbers from the pyramid she said, quietly, that as I did not want to know the answer, she would be much obliged if I would let her translate the cypher.

"With pleasure," I replied. "And I shall do so all the more willingly as I shall thereby save your delicacy from sharing with me a secret which may or may not be agreeable. I promise you not to try to find it out. It is enough for me to see you convinced."

"I shall be convinced when I have verified the truth of the reply."

"Are you persuaded, dearest Esther, that I have had nothing to do with framing this answer?"

"I shall be quite sure of it if it has spoken the truth, and if so the oracle will have conquered, for the matter is so secret a one that even I do not know of it. You need not know yourself, as it is only a trifle which would not interest you; but it will be enough to convince me that the answers of your oracle are dictated by an intelligence which has nothing in common with yours."

There was so much candour and frankness in what she said that a feeling of shame replaced the desire of deceiving her, and I shed some tears, which Esther could only interpret favourably to me. Nevertheless, they were tears of remorse, and now, as I write after such a lapse of years, I still regret having deceived one so worthy of my esteem and love. Even then I reproached myself, but a pitiable feeling of shame would not let me tell the truth; but I hated myself for thus leading astray one whose esteem I desired to gain.

In the mean time I was not absolutely sure that I had hit the mark, for in nature, like everything else, every law has its exceptions, and I might possibly have dug a pitfall for myself. On the other hand, if I were right, Esther would no doubt be convinced for the moment, but her belief would speedily disappear if she chanced to discover that the correspondence of moles on the human body was a necessary law of nature. In that case I could only anticipate her scorn. But however I might tremble I had carried the deception too far, and could not draw back.

I left Esther to call on Rigerboos, whom I thanked for his offices on my behalf with the chief of the police. He told me that I had nothing to fear from Piccolomini in Holland, but all the same he advised me not to go about without pistols. "I am on the eve of embarking for Batavia," said he, "in a vessel which I have laden with the ruins of my fortune. In the state my affairs are in I thought this the best plan. I have not insured the cargo, so as not diminish my profits, which will be considerable if I succeed. If the ship is taken or wrecked I shall take care not to survive its loss; and after all I shall not lose much."

Poor Riberboos said all this as if he were jesting, but despair had no doubt a good deal to do with his resolve, since it is only in great misery that we despise both life and fortune. The charming Therese Trenti, whom Rigerboos always spoke of as Our Lady, had contributed to his ruin in no small degree. She was then in London, where, by her own account, she was doing well. She had exchanged the name of Trenti for that of Cornelis, or Cornely, which, as I found out afterwards, was Rigerboo's real name. We spent an hour in writing to this curious woman, as we desired to take advantage of the circumstance that a man whom Rigerboos desired to commend to her was shortly going to England. When we had finished we went sleighing on the Amstel, which had been frozen over for several days. This diversion, of which the Dutch are very fond, is, to my thinking, the dullest imaginable, for an objectless journey is no pleasure to me. After we were well frozen we went to eat oysters, with Sillery, to warm ourselves again, and after that we went from one casino to another, not intending to commit any debauchery, but for want of something better to do; but it seemed decreed that whenever I preferred any amusement of this kind to the charms of Esther's society I should come to grief.

I do not know how it happened, but as we were going into one of these casinos Rigerboos called me loudly by my name, and at that instant a woman, such as one usually finds in these places, came forward and began to gaze at me. Although the room was ill enough lighted I saw it was the wretched Lucie, whom I had met a year before without her recognizing me. I turned away, pretending not to know her, for the sight of her was disagreeable to me, but in a sad voice she called me by my name, congratulating me on my prosperity and bewailing her own wretchedness. I saw that I could neither avoid her nor repulse her without inhumanity, so I called to Rigerboos to come upstairs and the girl would divert us by recounting the history of her life.

Strictly speaking, Lucie had not become ugly; one could still see that she had been a beautiful woman; but for all that her appearance inspired me with terror and disgust. Since the days when I had known her at Pasean, nineteen years of misery, profligacy, and shame had made her the most debased, the vilest creature that can be imagined. She told us her story at great length; the pith of it might be expressed in six lines.

The footman who had seduced her had taken her to Trieste to lie in, and the scoundrel lived on the sale of her charms for five or six months, and then a sea captain, who had taken a fancy to her, took her to Zante with the footman, who passed for her husband.

At Zante the footman turned soldier, and deserted the army four years after. She was left alone and continued living on the wages of prostitution for six years; but the goods she had to offer lowering in value, and her customers being of the inferior kind, she set out for England with a young Greek girl, whom an English officer of marines treated as his wife, and whom he abandoned in the streets of London when he got tired of her. After living for two or three years in the vilest haunts in London, Lucie came to Holland, where, not being able to sell her own person any longer, she became a procuress—a natural ending to her career. Lucie was only thirty-three, but she was the wreck of a woman, and women are always as old as they look.

While she told her history she emptied two bottles of Burgundy I had ordered, and which neither I nor my friend touched. Finally, she told us she was now supported by two pretty girls whom she kept, and who had to give her the half of what they got.

Rigerboos asked her, jokingly, if the girls were at the casino.

"No," said she, "they are not here, and shall never come here, for they are ladies of high birth, and their uncle, who looks after their interests, is a Venetian gentleman."

At this I could not keep back my laughter, but Lucie, without losing countenance, told me that she could only repeat the account they had given of themselves, that if we wanted to be convinced we had only to go and see them at a house she rented fifty paces off, and that we need not be afraid of being disturbed if we went, as their uncle lived in a different part of the town.

"Oh, indeed!" said I, "he does not live with his highborn nieces, then?"

"No, he only comes to dinner to hear how business has been going, and to take all the money from them."

"Come along," said Rigerboos, "we will go and see them."

As I was desirous of seeing and addressing the noble Venetian ladies of so honourable a profession, I told Lucie to take us to the house. I knew very well that the girls were impostors, and their gentleman-uncle a blackguard; but the die was cast.

We found them to be young and pretty. Lucie introduced me as a Venetian, and they were beside themselves with joy to have someone to whom they could talk. I found out directly that they came from Padua, not Venice, as they spoke the Paduan dialect, which I knew very well. I told them so, and they confessed it was the truth. I asked the name of their uncle, but they said they could not tell me.

"We can get on without knowing," said Rigerboos, catching hold of the one he liked best. Lucie brought in some ham, oysters, a pie, and a good many bottles of wine, and then left us.

I was not in the humour for wantonness, but Rigerboos was disposed to be merry; his sweetheart was at first inclined to be prudish on his taking liberties with her, but as I began to follow his example the ladies relaxed their severity; we went first to one and then the other, and before long they were both in the state of Eve before she used the fig-leaf.

After passing an hour in these lascivious combats we gave each of the girls four ducats, paid for the provisions we had consumed, and sent six Louis to Lucie. We then left them, I going to bed cross with myself for having engaged in such brutal pleasures.

Next morning I awoke late and in a bad humour, partly from the debauch of the night before (for profligacy depresses as well as degrades the mind) and partly from the thought that I had neglected Esther, who had unquestionably been grieved by my absence. I felt that I must hasten to reassure her, feeling certain that I should find some excuses to make, and that they would be well received. I rang for Le Duc, put on my dressing-gown, and sent him for my coffee. He had scarcely left the room when the door opened and I saw Perine and the fellow named Wiedan, whom I had seen at Piccolomini's, and who styled himself a friend of St. Germain. I was sitting on my bed, putting on my stockings. My apartments consisted of three fine rooms, but they were at the back of the house, and all the noise I could have made would not have been heard. The bell was on the other side of the room; Le Duc would be gone fully ten minutes, and I was in imminent danger of being assassinated without the possibility of self-defence.

The above thoughts flashed through my head with lightning speed, and all that I could do was to keep calm and say,

"Well, gentlemen, what can I do for you?" Wiedan took upon himself to answer me.

"Count Piccolomini has found himself forced to declare that he received the forged bill from us, in order that he may escape from the difficult position in which your denunciation placed him. He has warned us that he is going to do so, and we must escape forthwith if we want to avoid prosecution. We have not a penny; we are desperate men."

"Well, gentlemen, what have I to do with that?"

"Give us four hundred florins immediately; we do not want more, but we must have that much, and now. If you refuse we will take to flight with everything of yours that we can lay our hands on; and our arguments are these."

With this, each man drew a pistol from his pocket and aimed it at my head.

"You need not have recourse to violence," said I, "it can only be fatal to you. Stay, here are a hundred ducats more than you asked. Begone, and I wish you a pleasant journey, but I would not be here when my servant comes back if I were you."

Wiedan took the roll of money with a trembling hand and put it in his pocket without examining it; but Perine came up, and praising my noble generosity, would have put his arms around my neck and kissed me. I repulsed him, but without rudeness,

and they went their ways, leaving me very glad to have rid
myself of them at so cheap a rate.

As soon as I was out of this snare I rang my bell, not to have them
followed but that I might get dressed as quickly as possible. I did
not say a word to Le Duc about what had happened, I was silent
even to my landlord; and, after I had sent my Spaniard to M. d'O
to excuse my dining there that day, I went to the chief of police,
but had to wait two hours before I could see him. As soon as the
worthy man had heard my account of my misfortune he said he
would do his best to catch the two rascals, but he did not conceal
from me his fears that it was already too late.

I took the opportunity of telling him of Piccolomini's visit to me,
his claims and threats. He thanked me for doing so, and promised
to see to it; but he advised me for the future to be on my guard and
ready to defend myself in case I was attacked before he could place
my enemies in a place where they could do me no harm.

I hastened home again, as I felt ill. An acid taste in my mouth
skewed me how all these shocks had upset me; but I knew what to
do. I took a strong glass of lemonade, which made me bring up a
good deal of bile, and I then felt much better.

Towards evening I went to see Esther, and found her looking
serious and rather vexed; but as soon as she saw how pale I was her
face lighted up, and she asked me, in a voice of tenderest interest,
if I had been ill. I told her I had been out of sorts, that I had taken
some medicine, and that I now felt better.

"You will see my appetite at supper," added I, to calm her fears, "I have had nothing to eat since dinner yesterday."

This was really the truth, as I had only eaten a few oysters with the Paduan girls.

She could scarcely contain her joy at my recovery, and bade me kiss her, with which request I complied gladly, all unworthy though I felt of so great a favour.

"I am going to tell you an important piece of news," said she, "and that is that I am sure that you do not invent the answers to your oracle, or at least that you only do so when you choose. The reply you procured me was wonderful-nay, divine, for it told me of a secret unknown to all, even to myself. You may imagine my surprise when I convinced myself, with no little trouble of the truth of the answer.

"You possess a treasure, your oracle is infallible; but surely it can never lie, and my oracle tells me that you love me. It makes me glad to know that, for you are the man of my heart. But I want you to give me an exemplary proof of your love, and if you do love me you will not hesitate to do so. Stay, read the reply you got me; I am sure you do not know what it says; then I will tell you how you can make me quite happy."

I pretended to read, and kissed the words which declared I loved her. "I am delighted," said I, "that the oracle has convinced you so easily, but I must be excused if I say that I believe you knew as much long ago." She replied, blushing, that if it were possible to chew me the object in question I should not wonder at her ignorance. Then, coming to the proof of my love, she told me that she wanted me to communicate the secret to her. "You love me," said she, "and you ought to make no difficulty in assuring the bliss of a girl who will be your wife, and in your power. My father will agree to our marriage, and when I become your wife I will do whatever you please. We will even go and live in another country if that would add to your happiness. But you must teach me how to obtain the answer to any question without inventing it myself."

I took Esther's hands in mine; she inspired me with the tenderest feelings, and I kissed her hands with respectful fervour, saying, "You know, Esther, dear, that my word is passed at Paris. Certainly, Manon is not to be compared to you; but for all that I gave my promise to her poor mother, and I must keep it."

A sigh escaped from Esther, and her head fell upon her breast: but what could I do? I could not teach her any other way of consulting the oracle than the method she understood as well as I: my superiority over her only consisting in my greater craft and more extensive experience.

Early one morning, two or three days later, a man was announced as wanting to see me. He called himself an officer, but his name was perfectly unknown to me. I sent down to say that I could not see him, and as soon as my Spaniard went out I locked my door. What had happened already had made me suspicious, and I did not care to see any more gentlemen alone. The two scoundrels who had robbed me had eluded all the snares of the police, and Piccolomini was not to be found; but I knew a good many of the gang were still in Amsterdam, and I thought it well to be on my guard.

Some time after, Le Duc came in with a letter written in bad Italian, saying that it had been given him by an officer who was waiting for an answer. I opened it, and recognized the name I had heard a short while ago. The writer said we knew each other, but that he could only give his true name with his own lips, and that he had important information to give me.

I told Le Duc to shew him in, and to stay by the door. I saw enter a well-made man of about forty, dressed in the uniform of an officer of I do not know what army, and bearing on his countenance all the marks of an escaped gallows'-bird.

"What can I do for you, sir?" said I, as soon as he entered.

"Sir, we knew each other at Cerigo, sixteen or seventeen years ago, and I am delighted to have an opportunity of renewing the acquaintance."

I knew that I had spent but a few minutes at Cerigo, on my way to Constantinople, and concluded that my visitor must be one of the unfortunate wretches to whom I gave alms.

"Are you the man," I said, "who told me that you were the son of a Count
Peccini, of Padua, although there is no such count in Padua at all?"

"I congratulate you on your excellent memory," said he, coolly, "I am that very individual."

"Well, what do you want with me now?"

"I can't divulge my business in the presence of your servant."

"My servant does not understand Italian, so you can speak out; however, if you like, I will send him away."

I ordered Le Duc to stay in the ante-chamber, and when he had left the room my Paduan count told me that I had been with his nieces, and had treated them as if they were courtezans, and that he was come to demand satisfaction.

I was tired of being cheated, and I took hold of my pistols and pointed them at him, bidding him be gone instantly. Le Duc came in and the third robber took himself off, muttering that "a time would come."

I was placed in a disagreeable position; if I wanted to prosecute, I should have to tell the whole story to the police. I thought of my honour and determined to be silent, and the only person to whom I mentioned the matter was Rigerboos, who not being in the same position as myself took his measures, the result of which was that Lucie had to send her high-born dames about their business. But the wretched woman came to me to say that this misfortune had plunged her into the deepest distress, so I made her a present of a few ducats, and she went away somewhat consoled. I begged her not to call on me again.

Everything I did when I was away from Esther seemed to turn out ill, and I felt that if I wanted to be happy I should do well to keep near her; but my destiny, or rather my inconstancy, drew me away.

Three days afterwards, the villainous Major Sabi called on me to warn me to be on my guard, as, according to his account, a Venetian officer I had insulted and refused to give satisfaction to had vowed vengeance against me.

"Then," said I, "I shall have him arrested as an escaped galley slave, in which character I have given him alms, and for wearing without the right to do so the uniform of an officer, thereby disgracing the whole army. And pray what outrage can I have committed against girls who live in a brothel, and whom I have paid according to their deserts?"

"If what you say is true you are quite right, but this poor devil is in a desperate situation; he wants to leave the country, and does not possess a single florin. I advise you to give him an alms once more, and you will have done with him. Two score florins will not make you any the poorer, and will rid you of a villainous enemy."

"A most villainous one, I think." At last I agreed to give him the forty florins, and I handed them to him in a coffee-house where the major told me I should find him. The reader will see how I met this blackguard four months later.

Now, when all these troubles have been long over and I can think over them calmly, reflecting on the annoyances I experienced at Amsterdam, where I might have been so happy, I am forced to admit that we ourselves are the authors of almost all our woes and griefs, of which we so unreasonably complain. If I could live my life over again, should I be wiser? Perhaps; but then I should not be myself.

M. d'O—— asked me to sup with him at the Burgomasters' Lodge, and this was a great distinction, for, contrary to the rules of Freemasonry, no one but the twenty-four members who compose the lodge is admitted, and these twenty-four masons were the richest men on the Exchange.

"I have told them that you are coming," said M. d'O——, "and to welcome you more honourably the lodge will be opened in French." In short, these gentlemen gave me the most distinguished reception, and I had the fortune to make myself so agreeable to them that I was unanimously chosen an honorary member during the time I should stay at Amsterdam. As we were going away, M. d'O—— told me that I had supped with a company which represented a capital of three hundred millions.

Next day the worthy Dutchman begged me to oblige him by answering a question to which his daughter's oracle had replied in a very obscure manner. Esther encouraged me, and I asked what the question was. It ran as follows:

"I wish to know whether the individual who desires me and my company to transact a matter of the greatest importance is really a friend of the King of France?"

It was not difficult for me to divine that the Comte de St. Germain was meant. M. d'O was not aware that I knew him, and I had not forgotten what M. d'Afri had told me.

"Here's a fine opportunity," thought I, "for covering my oracle with glory, and giving my fair Esther something to think about."

I set to work, and after erecting my pyramid and placing above the four keys the letters O, S, A, D, the better to impose on Esther, I extracted the reply, beginning with the fourth key, D. The oracle ran as follows:

"The friend disavows. The order is signed. They grant. They refuse. All vanishes. Delay."

I pretended to think the reply a very obscure one, but Esther gave a cry of astonishment and declared that it gave a lot of information in an extraordinary style. M. d'O——, in an ecstasy of delight, exclaimed,

"The reply is clear enough for me. The oracle is divine; the word 'delay' is addressed to me. You and my daughter are clever enough in making the oracle speak, but I am more skilled than you in the interpretation thereof. I shall prevent the thing going any further. The project is no less a one than to lend a hundred millions, taking in pledge the diamonds of the French crown. The king wishes the loan to be concluded without the interference of his ministers and without their even knowing anything about it. I entreat you not to mention the matter to anyone."

He then went out.

"Now," said Esther, when we were by ourselves, "I am quite sure that that reply came from another intelligence than yours. In the name of all you hold sacred, tell me the meaning of those four letters, and why you usually omit them."

"I omit them, dearest Esther, because experience has taught me that in ordinary cases they are unnecessary; but while I was making the pyramid the command came to me to set them down, and I thought it well to obey."

"What do they mean?"

"They are the initial letters of the holy names of the cardinal intelligences of the four quarters of the world."

"I may not tell you, but whoever deals with the oracle should know them."

"Ah! do not deceive me; I trust in you, and it would be worse than murder to abuse so simple a faith as mine."

"I am not deceiving you, dearest Esther."

"But if you were to teach me the cabala, you would impart to me these holy names?"

"Certainly, but I cannot reveal them except to my successor. If I violate this command I should lose my knowledge; and this condition is well calculated to insure secrecy, is it not?"

"It is, indeed. Unhappy that I am, your successor will be, of course, Manon."

"No, Manon is not fitted intellectually for such knowledge as this."

"But you should fix on someone, for you are mortal after all. If you like, my father would give you the half of his immense fortune without your marrying me."

"Esther! what is it that you have said? Do you think that to possess you would be a disagreeable condition in my eyes?"

After a happy day—I think I may call it the happiest of my life—I left the too charming Esther, and went home towards the evening.

Three or four days after, M. d'O—— came into Esther's room, where he found us both calculating pyramids. I was teaching her to double, to triple, and to quadruple the cabalistic combinations. M. d'O—— strode into the room in a great hurry, striking his breast in a sort of ecstasy. We were surprised and almost frightened to see him so strangely excited, and rose to meet him, but he running up to us almost forced us to embrace him, which we did willingly.

"But what is the matter, papa dear?" said Esther, "you surprise me more than I can say."

"Sit down beside me, my dear children, and listen to your father and your best friend. I have just received a letter from one of the secretaries of their high mightinesses informing me that the French ambassador has demanded, in the name of the king his master, that the Comte St. Germain should be delivered over, and that the Dutch authorities have answered that His Most Christian Majesty's requests shall be carried out as soon as the person of the count can be secured. In consequence of this the police, knowing that the Comte St. Germain was staying at the Etoile d'Orient, sent to arrest him at midnight, but the bird had flown. The landlord declared that the count had posted off at nightfall, taking the way to Nimeguen. He has been followed, but there are small hopes of catching him up.

"It is not known how he can have discovered that a warrant existed against him, or how he continued to evade arrest."

"It is not known;" went an M. d'O——, laughing, "but everyone guesses that M. Calcoen, the same that wrote to me, let this friend of the French king's know that he would be wanted at midnight, and that if he did not get the key of the fields he would be arrested. He is not so foolish as to despise a piece of advice like that. The Dutch Government has expressed its sorrow to M. d'Afri that his excellence did not demand the arrest of St. Germain sooner, and the ambassador will not be astonished at this reply, as it is like many others given on similar occasions.

"The wisdom of the oracle has been verified, and I congratulate myself on having seized its meaning, for we were on the point of giving him a hundred thousand florins on account, which he said he must have immediately. He gave us in pledge the finest of the crown diamonds, and this we still retain. But we will return it to him on demand, unless it is claimed by the ambassador. I have never seen a finer stone.

"And now, my children, you see what I owe to the oracle. On the Exchange the whole company can do nothing but express their gratitude to me. I am regarded as the most prudent and most farseeing man in Holland. To you, my dear children, I owe this honour, but I wear my peacock's feathers without scruple.

"My dear Casanova, you will dine with us, I hope. After dinner I shall beg you to enquire of your inscrutable intelligence whether we ought to declare ourselves in possession of the splendid diamond, or to observe secrecy till it is reclaimed."

After this discourse papa embraced us once more and left us.

"Sweetheart," said Esther, throwing her arms round my neck, "you have an opportunity for giving me a strong proof of your friendship. It will cost you nothing, but it will cover me with honour and happiness."

"Command me, and it shall be done. You cannot think that I would refuse you a favour which is to cost me nothing, when I should deem myself happy to shed my blood for your sake."

"My father wishes you to tell him after dinner whether it will be better to declare that they have the diamond or to keep silence till it is claimed. When he asks you a second time, tell him to seek the answer of me, and offer to consult the oracle also, in case my answer may be too obscure. Then perform the operation, and I will make my father love me all the better, when he sees that my knowledge is equal to yours."

"Dearest one, would I not do for thee a task a thousand times more difficult than this to prove my love and my devotion? Let us set to work. Do you write the question, set up the pyramids, and inscribe with your own hand the all-powerful initials. Good. Now begin to extract the answer by means of the divine key. Never was a cleverer pupil!"

When all this had been done, I suggested the additions and subtractions I wanted made, and she was quite astonished to read the following reply: "Silence necessary. Without silence, general derision. Diamond valueless; mere paste."

I thought she would have gone wild with delight. She laughed and laughed again.

"What an amazing reply!" said she. "The diamond is false, and it is I who am about to reveal their folly to them. I shall inform my father of this important secret. It is too much, it overwhelms me; I can scarcely contain myself for joy! How much I owe you, you wonderful and delightful man! They will verify the truth of the oracle immediately, and when it is found that the famous diamond is but glittering paste the company will adore my father, for it will feel that but for him it would have been covered with shame, by avowing itself the dupe of a sharper. Will you leave the pyramid with me?"

"Certainly; but it will not teach you anything you do not know." The father came in again and we had dinner, and after the dessert, when the worthy d 'O—— learnt from his daughter's oracle that the stone was false, the scene became a truly comical one. He burst into exclamations of astonishment, declared the thing impossible, incredible, and at last begged me to ask the same question, as he was quite sure that his daughter was mistaken, or rather that the oracle was deluding her.

I set to work, and was not long in obtaining my answer. When he saw that it was to the same effect as Esther's, though differently expressed, he had no longer any doubts as to his daughter's skill, and hastened to go and test the pretended diamond, and to advise his associates to say nothing about the matter after they had received proofs of the worthlessness of the stone. This advice was, as it happened, useless; for though the persons concerned said nothing, everybody knew about it, and people said, with their usual malice, that the dupes had been duped most thoroughly, and that St. Germain had pocketed the hundred thousand florins; but this was not the case.

Esther was very proud of her success, but instead of being satisfied with what she had done, she desired more fervently every day to possess the science in its entirety, as she supposed I possessed it.

It soon became known that St. Germain had gone by Emden and had embarked for England, where he had arrived in safety. In due time we shall hear some further details concerning this celebrated impostor; and in the meanwhile I must relate a catastrophe of another kind, which was near to have made me die the death of a fool.

It was Christmas Day. I had got up early in the morning in better spirits than usual. The old women tell you that always presages misfortune, but I was as far then as I am now from making my happiness into an omen of grief. But this time chance made the foolish belief of good effect. I received a letter and a large packet from Paris; they came from Manon. I opened the letter and I thought I should have died of grief when I read,—

"Be wise, and receive the news I give you calmly. The packet contains your portrait and all the letters you have written to me. Return me my portrait, and if you have kept my letters be kind enough to burn them. I rely on your honour. Think of me no more. Duty bids me do all I can to forget you, for at this hour to-morrow I shall become the wife of M. Blondel of the Royal Academy, architect to the king. Please do not seem as if you knew me if we chance to meet on your return to Paris."

This letter struck me dumb with astonishment, and for more than two hours after I read it I was, as it were, bereft of my senses. I sent word to M. d'O—— that, not feeling well, I was going to keep my room all day. When I felt a little better I opened the packet. The first thing to fall out was my portrait. I looked at it, and such was the perturbation of my mind, that, though the miniature really represented me as of a cheerful and animated expression, I thought I beheld a dreadful and a threatening visage. I went to my desk and wrote and tore up a score of letters in which I overwhelmed the faithless one with threats and reproaches.

I could bear no more; the forces of nature were exhausted, and I was obliged to lie down and take a little broth, and court that sleep which refused to come. A thousand designs came to my disordered imagination. I rejected them one by one, only to devise new ones. I would slay this Blondel, who had carried off a woman who was mine and mine only; who was all but my wife. Her treachery should be punished by her losing the object for whom she had deserted me. I accused her father, I cursed her brother for having left me in ignorance of the insult which had so traitorously been put upon me.

I spent the day and night in these delirious thoughts, and in the morning, feeling worse than ever, I sent to M. d'O—— to say that I could not possibly leave my room. Then I began to read and re-read the letters I had written to Manon, calling upon her name in a sort of frenzy; and again set myself to write to her without finishing a single letter. The emptiness of my stomach and the shock I had undergone began to stupefy me, and for a few moments I forgot my anguish only to re-awaken to acuter pains soon after.

About three o'clock, the worthy M. d'O—— came to invite me to go with him to the Hague, where the chief masons of Holland met on the day following to keep the Feast of St. John, but when he saw my condition he did not press me to come.

"What is the matter with you, my dear Casanova?" said he.

"I have had a great grief, but let us say no more about it."

He begged me to come and see Esther, and left me looking almost as downcast as I was. However, the next morning Esther anticipated my visit, for at nine o'clock she and her governess came into the room. The sight of her did me good. She was astonished to see me so undone and cast down, and asked me what was the grief of which I had spoken to her father, and which had proved too strong for my philosophy.

"Sit down beside me, Esther dear, and allow me to make a mystery of what has affected me so grievously. Time, the mighty healer, and still more your company, will effect a cure which I should in vain seek by appealing to my reason. Whilst we talk of other things I shall not feel the misfortune which gnaws at my heart."

"Well, get up, dress yourself, and come and spend the day with me, and I will do my best to make you forget your sorrow."

"I feel very weak; for the last three days I have only taken a little broth and chocolate."

At these words her face fell, and she began to weep.

After a moment's silence she went to my desk, took a pen, and wrote a few lines, which she brought to me. They were,—

"Dear, if a large sum of money, beyond what my father owes you, can remove or even soothe your grief I can be your doctor, and you ought to know that your accepting my treatment would make me happy."

I took her hands and kissed them affectionately, saying,—

"No, dear Esther, generous Esther, it is not money I want, for if I did I would ask you and your father as a friend: what I want, and what no one can give me, is a resolute mind, and determination to act for the best."

"Ask advice of your oracle."

I could not help laughing.

"Why do you laugh?" said she, "if I am not mistaken, the oracle must know a remedy for your woes."

"I laughed, dearest, because I felt inclined to tell you to consult the oracle this time. As for me I will have nothing to do with it, lest the cure be worse than the disease."

"But you need not follow your advice unless you like it."

"No, one is free to act as one thinks fit; but not to follow the advice of the oracle would be a contempt of the intelligence which directs it."

Esther could say no more, and stood silent for several minutes, and then said that if I like she would stay with me for the rest of the day. The joy which illumined my countenance was manifest, and I said that if she would stay to dinner I would get up, and no doubt her presence would give me an appetite. "Ah!" said she, "I will make you the dish you are so fond of." She ordered the sedan-chairs to be sent back, and went to my landlady to order an appetising repast, and to procure the chafing-dish and the spirits of wine she required for her own cooking.

Esther was an angel, a treasure, who consented to become mine if I would communicate to her a science which did not exist. I felt that I was looking forward to spending a happy day; this shewed me that I could forget Manon, and I was delighted with the idea. I got out of bed, and when Esther came back and found me on my feet she gave a skip of pleasure. "Now," said she, "you must oblige me by dressing, and doing your hair as if you were going to a ball."

"That," I answered, "is a funny idea, but as it pleases you it pleases me."

I rang for Le Duc, and told him I wanted to have my hair done, and to be dressed as if I were going to a ball. "Choose the dress that suits me best."

"No," said Esther, "I will choose it myself."

Le Duc opened my trunk, and leaving her to rummage in it he came to shave me, and to do my hair. Esther, delighted with her task, called in the assistance of her governess. She put on my bed a lace shirt, and the suit she found most to her taste. Then coming close, as if to see whether Le Duc was dressing my hair properly, she said,

"A little broth would do you good; send for a dish, it will give you an appetite for dinner."

I thought her advice dictated by the tenderest care, and I determined to benefit by it. So great was the influence of this charming girl over me, that, little by little, instead of loving Manon, I hated her. That gave me courage, and completed my cure. At the present time I can see that Manon was very wise in accepting Blondel's offer, and that my love for self and not my love for her was wounded.

I was in my servant's hands, my face turned away towards the fire, so that I could not see Esther, but only divert myself with the idea that she was inspecting my belongings, when all at once she presented herself with a melancholy air, holding Mamon's fatal letter in her hand.

"Am I to blame," said she, timidly, "for having discovered the cause of your sorrow?"

I felt rather taken aback, but looking kindly at her, I said,

"No, no, my dear Esther; pity your friend, and say no more about it."

"Then I may read all the letters?"

"Yes, dearest, if it will amuse you."

All the letters of the faithless Manon Baletti to me, with mine to her, were together on my table. I pointed them out to Esther, who begun to read them quite eagerly.

When I was dressed, as if for some Court holiday, Le Duc went out and left us by ourselves, for the worthy governess, who was working at her lace by the window, looked at her lace, and nothing else. Esther said that nothing had ever amused her so much as those letters.

"Those cursed epistles, which please you so well, will be the death of me."

"Death? Oh, no! I will cure you, I hope."

"I hope so, too; but after dinner you must help me to burn them all from first to last."

"Burn them! No; make me a present of them. I promise to keep them carefully all my days."

"They are yours, Esther. I will send them to you to-morrow."

These letters were more than two hundred in number, and the shortest were four pages in length. She was enchanted to find herself the possessor of the letters, and she said she would make them into a parcel and take them away herself.

"Shall you send back the portrait to your faithless mistress?" said she.

"I don't know what to do with it."

"Send it back to her; she is not worthy of your honouring her by keeping it. I am sure that your oracle would give you the same advice. Where is the portrait? Will you shew it me?"

I had the portrait in the interior of a gold snuff-box, but I had never shewn it to Esther for fear she should think Manon handsomer than herself, and conclude that I only shewd it her out of vanity; but as she now asked to see it I opened the box where it was and gave it her.

Any other woman besides Esther would have pronounced Manon downright ugly, or have endeavored at the least to find some fault with her, but Esther pronounced her to be very beautiful, and only said it was a great pity so fair a body contained so vile a soul.

The sight of Manon's portrait made Esther ask to see all the other portraits which Madame Manzoni had sent me from Venice. There were naked figures amongst them, but Esther was too pure a spirit to put on the hateful affectations of the prude, to whom everything natural is an abomination. O-Murphy pleased her very much, and her history, which I related, struck her as very curious. The portrait of the fair nun, M—— M——, first in the habit of her order and afterwards naked, made her laugh, but I would not tell Esther her story, in spite of the lively desire she displayed to hear it.

At dinner-time a delicate repast was brought to us, and we spent two delightful hours in the pleasures of a conversation and the table. I seemed to have passed from death to life, and Esther was delighted to have been my physician. Before we rose from table I had declared my intention of sending Manon's portrait to her husband on the day following, but her good nature found a way of dissuading me from doing so without much difficulty.

Some time after, while we were talking in front of the fire, she took a piece of paper, set up the pyramids, and inscribed the four keys O, S, A, D. She asked if I should send the portrait to the husband, or whether it would not be more generous to return it to the faithless Manon. Whilst she was calculating she said over and over again, with a smile, "I have not made up the answer." I pretend to believe her, and we laughed like two augurs meeting each other alone. At last the reply came that I ought to return the portrait, but to the giver, since to send it to the husband would be an act unworthy of a man of honour.

I praised the wisdom of the oracle, and kissed the Pythoness a score of times, promising that the cabala should be obeyed implicitly, adding that she had no need of being taught the science since she knew it as well as the inventor.

I spoke the truth, but Esther laughed, and, fearing lest I should really think so, took pains to assure me of the contrary.

It is thus that love takes his pleasure, thus his growth increases, and thus that he so soon becomes a giant in strength.

"Shall I be impertinent," said Esther, "if I ask you where your portrait is? Manon says in her letter that she is sending it back; but I don't see it anywhere."

"In my first paroxysm of rage, I threw it down; I don't know in what direction. What was thus despised by her cannot be of much value to me."

"Let us look for it; I should like to see it."

We soon found it on my table, in the midst of a of books; Esther said it was a speaking likeness.

"I would give it you if such a present were worthy of you."

"Ah! you could not give me anything I would value more."

"Will you deign to accept it, Esther, though it has been possessed by another?"

"It will be all the dearer to me."

At last she had to leave me, after a day which might be called delightful if happiness consists of calm and mutual joys without the tumultuous raptures of passion. She went away at ten, after I had promised to spend the whole of the next day with her.

After an unbroken sleep of nine hours' duration I got up refreshed and feeling once more in perfect health, and I went to see Esther immediately. I found she was still abed and asleep, but her governess went and roused her in spite of my request that her repose should be respected.

She received me with a sweet smile as she sat up in bed, and shewd me my voluminous correspondence with Manon on her night-table, saying that she had been reading it till two o'clock in the morning.

Her appearance was ravishing. A pretty cambric night-cap, tied with a light-blue ribbon and ornamented with lace, set off the beauties of her face; and a light shawl of Indian muslin, which she had hastily thrown on, veiled rather than concealed her snowy breast, which would have shamed the works of Praxiteles. She allowed me to take a hundred kisses on her rosy lips—ardent kisses which the sight of such charms made yet more ardent; but her hands forbade my approach to those two spheres I so longed to touch.

I sat down by her and told her that her charms of body and mind would make a man forget all the Manons that ever were.

"Is your Marion fair to see all over?" said she.

"I really can't say, for, not being her husband, I never had an opportunity of investigating the matter."

"Your discretion is worthy of all praise," she said, with a smile, "such conduct becomes a man of delicate feeling."

"I was told by her nurse that she was perfect in all respects, and that no mote or blemish relieved the pure whiteness of her skin."

"You must have a different notion of me?"

"Yes, Esther, as the oracle revealed to me the great secret you desired to know. Nevertheless, I should find you perfect in all your parts."

Hereupon I was guilty of a stupidity which turned to my confusion. I said,

"If I became your husband, I could easily refrain from touching you there."

"I suppose you think," said she, blushing, and evidently a little vexed, "that if you touched it your desires might be lessened?"

This question probed me to the core and covered me with shame. I burst into tears, and begged her pardon in so truly repentant a voice that sympathy made her mingle her tears with mine. The incident only increased our intimacy, for, as I kissed her tears away, the same desires consumed us, and if the voice of prudence had not intervened, doubtless all would have been over. As it was, we had but a foretaste and an earnest of that bliss which it was in our power to procure. Three hours seemed to us as many minutes. She begged me to go into her sitting-room while she dressed, and we then went down and dined with the wretched secretary, who adored her, whom she did not love, and who must have borne small love to me, seeing how high I stood in her graces.

We passed the rest of the day together in that confidential talk which is usual when the foundations of the most intimate friendship have been laid between two persons of opposite sex, who believe themselves created for each other. Our flames burnt as brightly, but with more restraint, in the dining-room as in the bedroom. In the very air of the bedroom of a woman one loves there is something so balmy and voluptuous that the lover, asked to choose between this garden of delights and Paradise, would not for one moment hesitate in his choice.

We parted with hearts full of happiness, saying to each other, "Till to-morrow."

I was truly in love with Esther, for my sentiment for her was composed of sweeter, calmer, and more lively feelings than mere sensual love, which is ever stormy and violent. I felt sure I could persuade her to marry me without my first teaching her what could not be taught. I was sorry I had not let her think herself as clever as myself in the cabala, and I feared it would be impossible to undeceive her without exciting her to anger, which would cast out love. Nevertheless, Esther was the only woman who would make me forget Manon, whom I began to think unworthy of all I had proposed doing for her.

M. d'O—— came back and I went to dine with him. He was pleased to hear that his daughter had effected a complete cure by spending a day with me. When we were alone he told me that he had heard at the Hague that the Comte St. Germain had the art of making diamonds which only differed from the real ones in weight, and which, according to him, would make his fortune. M. d'O—— would have been amused if I had told him all I knew about this charlatan.

Next day I took Esther to the concert, and while we were there she told me that on the day following she would not leave her room, so that we could talk about getting married without fear of interruption. This was the last day of the year 1759.

CHAPTER XI

The appointment which Esther had made with me would probably have serious results; and I felt it due to my honour not to deceive her any longer, even were it to cost me my happiness; however, I had some hope that all would turn out well.

I found her in bed, and she told me that she intended to stop there throughout the day. I approved, for in bed I thought her ravishing.

"We will set to work," said she; and her governess set a little table by her bed, and she gave me a piece of paper covered with questions tending to convince me that before I married her I should communicate to her my supposed science. All these questions were artfully conceived, all were so worded as to force the oracle to order me to satisfy her, or to definitely forbid my doing so. I saw the snare, and all my thoughts were how to avoid it, though I pretended to be merely considering the questions. I could not make the oracle speak to please Esther, and I could still less make it pronounce a positive prohibition, as I feared that she would resent such an answer bitterly and revenge herself on me. Nevertheless, I had to assume an indifferent air, and I got myself out of the difficulty by equivocal answers, till the good-humoured papa came to summon me to dinner.

He allowed his daughter to stay in bed on the condition that she was to do no more work, as he was afraid that by applying herself so intently she would increase her headache. She promised, much to my delight, that he should be obeyed, but on my return from dinner I found her asleep, and sitting at her bedside I let her sleep on.

When she awoke she said she would like to read a little; and as if by inspiration, I chanced to take up Coiardeau's 'Heroides', and we inflamed each other by reading the letters of Heloise and Abelard. The ardours thus aroused passed into our talk and we began to discuss the secret which the oracle had revealed.

"But, Esther dear," said I, "did not the oracle reveal a circumstance of which you knew perfectly well before?"

"No, sweetheart, the secret was perfectly unknown to me and would have continued unknown."

"Then you have never been curious enough to inspect your own person?"

"However curious I may have been, nature placed that mole in such a position as to escape any but the most minute search."

"You have never felt it, then?"

"It is too small to be felt."

"I don't believe it."

She allowed my hand to wander indiscreetly, and my happy fingers felt all the precincts of the temple of love. This was enough to fire the chastest disposition. I could not find the object of my research, and, not wishing to stop short at so vain an enjoyment, I was allowed to convince myself with my eyes that it actually existed. There, however, her concessions stopped short, and I had to content myself by kissing again and again all those parts which modesty no longer denied to my gaze.

Satiated with bliss, though I had not attained to the utmost of enjoyment, which she wisely denied me, after two hours had been devoted to those pastimes which lead to nothing, I resolved to tell her the whole truth and to shew her how I had abused her trust in me, though I feared that her anger would be roused.

Esther, who had a large share of intelligence (indeed if she had had less I could not have deceived her so well), listened to me without interrupting me and without any signs of anger or astonishment. At last, when I had brought my long and sincere confession to an end, she said,

"I know your love for me is as great as mine for you; and if I am certain that what you have just said cannot possibly be true, I am forced to conclude that if you do not communicate to me all the secrets of your science it is because to do so is not in your power. Let us love one another till death, and say no more about this matter."

After a moment's silence, she went on,—

"If love has taken away from you the courage of sincerity I forgive you, but I am sorry for you. You have given me too positive proof of the reality of your science to be able to shake my belief. You could never have found out a thing of which I myself was ignorant, and of which no mortal man could know."

"And if I shew you, Esther dear, that I knew you had this mole, that I had good reasons for supposing you to be ignorant of it, will your belief be shaken then?"

"You knew it? How could you have seen it? It's incredible!"

"I will tell you all."

I then explained to her the theory of the correspondence of moles on the various parts of the human body, and to convince her I ended by saying that her governess who had a large mark on her right cheek ought to have one very like it on her left thigh. At this she burst into laughter, and said, "I will find out, but after all you have told me I can only admire you the more for knowing what no one else does."

"Do you really think, Esther, that I am the sole possessor of this science? Undeceive yourself. All who have studied anatomy, physiology, and astrology, know of it."

"Then I beg you to get me, by to-morrow—yes, tomorrow—all the books which will teach me secrets of that nature. I long to be able to astonish the ignorant with my cabala, which I see requires a mixture of knowledge and imposition. I wish to devote myself entirely to this study. We can love each other to the death, but we can do that without getting married."

I re-entered my lodging in a peaceful and happy frame of mind; an enormous weight seemed taken off my spirits. Next morning I purchased such volumes as I judged would instruct and amuse her at the same time, and went to present them to her. She was most pleased with my Conis, as she found in it the character of truth. As she wished to shine by her answers through the oracle it was necessary for her to have an extensive knowledge of science, and I put her on the way.

About that time I conceived the idea of making a short tour in Germany before returning to Paris, and Esther encouraged me to do so, after I had promised that she should see me again before the end of the year. This promise was sincerely, given; and though from that day to this I have not beheld the face of that charming and remarkable woman, I cannot reproach myself with having deceived her wilfully, for subsequent events prevented me from keeping my word.

I wrote to M. d'Afri requesting him to procure me a passport through the empire, where the French and other belligerent powers were then campaigning. He answered very politely that I had no need of a passport, but that if I wished to have one he would send it me forthwith. I was content with this letter and put it among my papers, and at Cologne it got me a better reception than all the passports in the world.

I made M. d'O—— the depositary of the various moneys I had in different banking houses, and the worthy man, who was a true friend to me, gave me a bill of exchange on a dozen of the chief houses in Germany.

When my affairs were all in order I started in my post-chaise, with the sum of nearly a hundred thousand Dutch florins to my credit, some valuable jewels, and a well-stocked wardrobe. I sent my Swiss servant back to Paris, keeping only my faithful Spaniard, who on this occasion travelled with me, seated behind my chaise.

Thus ends the history of my second visit to Holland, where I did nothing to augment my fortune. I had some unpleasant experiences there for which I had my own imprudence to thank, but after the lapse of so many years I feel that these mishaps were more than compensated by the charms of Esther's society.

I only stopped one day at Utrecht, and two days after I reached Cologne at noon, without accident, but not without danger, for at a distance of half a league from the town five deserters, three on the right hand and two on the left, levelled their pistols at me, with the words, "Your money or your life." However, I covered the postillion with my own pistol, threatening to fire if he did not drive on, and the robbers discharged their weapons at the carriage, not having enough spirit to shoot the postillion.

If I had been like the English, who carry a light purse for the benefit of the highwaymen, I would have thrown it to these poor wretches; but, as it was, I risked my life rather than be robbed. My

Spaniard was quite astonished not to have been struck by any of the balls which whistled past his ears.

The French were in winter quarters at Cologne, and I put up at the "Soleil d'Or." As I was going in, the first person I met was the Comte de Lastic, Madame d'Urfe's nephew, who greeted me with the utmost politeness, and offered to take me to M. de Torci, who was in command. I accepted, and this gentleman was quite satisfied with the letter M. d'Afri had written me. I told him what had happened to me as I was coming into Cologne, and he congratulated me on the happy issue of the affair, but with a soldier's freedom blamed the use I had made of my courage.

"You played high," said he, "to save your money, but you might have lost a limb, and nothing would have made up for that."

I answered that to make light of a danger often diminished it. We laughed at this, and he said that if I was going to make any stay in Cologne I should probably have the pleasure of seeing the highwaymen hanged.

"I intend to go to-morrow," said I, "and if anything could keep me at Cologne it would certainly not be the prospect of being present at an execution, as such sights are not at all to my taste."

I had to accept M. de Lastic's invitation to dinner, and he persuaded me to go with himself and his friend, M. de Flavacour, an officer of high rank, and an agreeable man, to the theatre. As I felt sure that I should be introduced to ladies, and wished to make something of a figure, I spent an hour in dressing.

I found myself in a box opposite to a pretty woman, who looked at me again and again through her opera-glass. That was enough to rouse my curiosity, and I begged M. de Lastic to introduce me; which he did with the best grace imaginable. He first presented me to Count Kettler, lieutenant-general in the Austrian army, and on the general staff of the French army—just as the French General Montacet was on the staff of the Austrian army. I was then presented to the lady whose beauty had attracted my attention the moment I entered my box. She greeted me graciously, and asked me questions about Paris and Brussels, where she had been educated, without appearing to pay any attention to my replies, but gazing at my lace and jewellery.

While we were talking of indifferent matters, like new acquaintances, she suddenly but politely asked me if I intended to make a long stay in Cologne.

"I think of crossing the Rhine to-morrow," I answered, "and shall probably dine at Bonn."

This reply, which was given as indifferently as her question, appeared to vex her; and I thought her vexation a good omen. General Kettler then rose, saying,—

"I am sure, sir, that this lady will persuade you to delay your departure—at least, I hope so, that I may bane the pleasure of seeing more of your company."

I bowed and he went out with Lastic, leaving me alone with this ravishing beauty. She was the burgomaster's wife, and the general was nearly always with her.

"Is the count right," said she, pleasantly, "in attributing such power to me?"

"I think so, indeed," I answered, "but he may possibly be wrong in thinking you care to exercise it."

"Very good! We must catch him, then, if only as the punishment of his indiscretion. Stay."

I was so astonished at this speech that I looked quite foolish and had to collect my senses. I thought the word indiscretion sublime, punishment exquisite, and catching admirable; and still more the idea of catching him by means of me. I thought it would be a mistake to enquire any further, and putting on an expression of resignation and gratitude I lowered my lips and kissed her hand with a mixture of respect and sentiment, which, without exactly imparting my feelings for her, let her know that they might be softened without much difficulty.

"Then you will stay, sir! It is really very kind of you, for if you went off to-morrow people might say that you only came here to shew your disdain for us. Tomorrow the general gives a ball, and I hope you will be one of the party."

"Can I hope to dance with you all the evening?"

"I promise to dance with nobody but you, till you get tired of me."

"Then we shall dance together through all the ball."

"Where did you get that pomade which perfumes the air? I smelt it as soon as you came into the box."

"It came from Florence, and if you do not like it you shall not be troubled with it any more."

"Oh! but I do like it. I should like some of it myself."

"And I shall be only too happy if you will permit me to send you a little to-morrow."

Just then the door of the box opened and the entrance of the general prevented her from replying. I was just going, when the count said:

"I am sure madame has prevailed on you to stay, and to come to my ball and supper to-morrow?"

"She has led me to anticipate that you would do me that honour, and she promises to dance the quadrilles with me. How can one resist entreaty from such lips?"

"Quite so, and I am obliged to her for having kept you with us. I hope to see you to-morrow."

I went out of the box in love, and almost happy in anticipation. The pomade was a present from Esther, and it was the first time I had used it. The box contained twenty-four pots of beautiful china. The next day I put twelve into an elegant casket, which I wrapped up in oil-cloth and sent to her without a note.

I spent the morning by going over Cologne with a guide; I visited all the
marvels of the place, and laughed with all my heart to see the horse Bayard, of whom Ariosto has sung, ridden by the four sons of

Aimon, or Amone, father of Bradamante the Invincible, and Ricciardetto the Fortunate.

I dined with M. de Castries, and everybody was surprised that the general had asked me himself to the ball, as his jealousy was known, while the lady was supposed only to suffer his attentions through a feeling of vanity. The dear general was well advanced in years, far from good-looking, and as his mental qualities by no means compensated for his lack of physical ones he was by no means an object to inspire love. In spite of his jealousy, he had to appear pleased that I sat next the fair at supper, and that I spent the night in dancing with her or talking to her. It was a happy night for me, and I re-entered my lodging no longer thinking of leaving Cologne. In a moment of ecstasy, emboldened by the turn the conversation had taken, I had dared to tell her that if she would meet me alone I would stay in Cologne till the end of the carnival. "And what would you say," she asked, "if I give my promise, and do not keep it?"

"I should bemoan my lot, without accusing you; I should say to myself that you had found it impossible to keep your word."

"You are very good; you must stay with us."

The day after the ball I went to pay her my first visit. She made me welcome, and introduced me to her worthy husband, who, though neither young nor handsome, was extremely good-hearted. After I had been there an hour, we heard the general's carriage coming, and she said to me:

"If he asks you whether you are going to the Elector's ball at Bonn, say yes!"

The general came in, and after the usual compliments had been passed I withdrew.

I did not know by whom the ball was to be given, or when it was to take place, but scenting pleasure from afar off I hastened to make enquiries about it, and heard that all the good families in Cologne were going. It was a masked ball, and consequently open to all. I decided then that I would go; indeed I concluded that I had had orders to that effect, and at all events my lady would be there, and I might hope for a happy meeting with her. But as I wished to keep up my incognito as much as possible, I resolved to reply to all who asked me that important business would prevent my being present.

It fell out that the general asked me this very question in the presence of the lady, and without regard to the orders I had received from her I replied that my health would forbid my having that pleasure.

"You are very wise, sir," said the general, "all the pleasures on earth should be sacrificed when it is a question of one's health."

I think so, too, now, but I thought differently then.

On the day of the ball, towards the evening, I set out in a post-chaise, disguised so that not a soul in Cologne could have recognized me, and provided with a box containing two dominoes; and on my arrival at Bonn I took a room and put on one of the dominoes, locking up the other in the box; and I then had myself carried to the ball in a sedan-chair.

I got in easily and unperceived, and recognized all the ladies of Cologne without their masks, and my mistress sitting at a faro-table risking a ducat. I was glad to see in the banker, Count Verita of Verona, whom I had known in Bavaria. He was in the Elector's service. His small bank did not contain more than five or six ducats, and the punters, men and women, were not more than twelve. I took up a position by my mistress, and the banker asked me to cut. I excused myself with a gesture, and my neighbour cut without being asked. I put ten ducats on a single card, and lost four times running; I played at the second deal, and experienced the same fate. At the third deal nobody would cut, and the general, who was standing by but not playing, agreed to do so. I fancied his cutting would be lucky, and I put fifty ducats on one card. I won. I went 'paroli', and at the second deal I broke the bank. Everybody was curious about me; I was stared at and followed, but seizing a favourable opportunity I made my escape.

I went to my room, took out my money, changed my costume, and returned to the ball. I saw the table occupied by new gamesters, and another banker who seemed to have a good deal of gold, but not caring to play any more I had not brought much money with me. I mingled in all the groups in the ballroom, and on all sides I heard expressions of curiosity about the mask who broke the first bank.

I did not care to satisfy the general curiosity, but made my way from one side of the room to the other till I found the object of my search talking to Count Verita, and as I drew near I found out that they were talking of me. The count was saying that the Elector had been asking who had broken the bank, and that General Kettler had expressed his opinion that it was a Venetian who had been in Cologne for the last week. My mistress answered that she did not think I was there, as she had heard me say that the state of my health would keep me at home.

"I know Casanova," said the count, "and if he be at Bonn the Elector shall hear of it, and he shan't go off without my seeing him." I saw that I might easily be discovered after the ball, but I defied the keenest eyes to penetrate beneath my present disguise. I should have, no doubt, remained unknown, but when the quadrilles were being arranged I took my place in one, without reflecting that I should have to take off my mask.

As soon as my mistress saw me she told me she had been deceived, as she would have wagered that I was the masker who broke Count Verita's bank. I told her I had only just come.

At the end of the dance the count spied me out and said, "My dear fellow-countryman, I am sure you are the man who broke my bank; I congratulate you."

"I should congratulate myself if I were the fortunate individual."

"I am sure that it was you."

I left him laughing, and after having taken some refreshments I continued dancing. Two hours afterwards the count saw me again and said,—

"You changed your domino in such a room, in such a house. The Elector knows all about it, and as a punishment for this deceit he has ordered me to tell you that you are not to leave Bonn to-morrow."

"Is he going to arrest me, then?"

"Why not, if you refuse his invitation to dinner tomorrow?"

"Tell his highness that his commands shall be obeyed. Will you present me to him now?"

"He has left the ball, but wait on me to-morrow at noon." So saying, he gave me his hand and went away.

I took care to keep the appointment on the day following, but when I was presented I was in some confusion, as the Elector was surrounded by five or six courtiers, and never having seen him I looked in vain for an ecclesiastic. He saw my embarrassment and hastened to put an end to it, saying, in bad Venetian, "I am wearing the costume of Grand Master of the Teutonic Order to-day." In spite of his costume I made the usual genuflexion, and when I would have kissed his hand he would not allow it, but shook mine in an affectionate manner. "I was at Venice," said he, "when you were under the Leads, and my nephew, the Elector of Bavaria, told me that after your fortunate escape you stayed some time at Munich; if you had come to Cologne I should have kept you. I hope that after dinner you will be kind enough to tell us the story of your escape, that you will stay to supper, and will join in a little masquerade with which we propose to amuse ourselves."

I promised to tell my tale if he thought it would not weary him, warning him that it would take two hours. "One could never have too much of a good thing," he was kind enough to say; and I made him laugh by my account of the conversation between the Duc de Choiseul and myself.

At dinner the prince spoke to me in Venetian, and was pleased to be most gracious towards me. He was a man of a jovial and easy-going disposition, and with his look of health one would not have prophesied so soon an end as came to him. He died the year following.

As soon as we rose from table he begged me to begin my story, and for two hours I had the pleasure of keeping this most brilliant company amused.

My readers know the history; its interest lies in the dramatic nature of the details, but it is impossible to communicate the fire of a well-told story to an account in writing.

The Elector's little ball was very pleasant. We were all dressed as peasants, and the costumes were taken from a special wardrobe of the prince's. It would have been ridiculous to choose any other dresses, as the Elector wore one of the same kind himself. General Kettler was the best disguised of us all; he looked the rustic to the life. My mistress was ravishing. We only danced quadrilles and German dances. There were only four or five ladies of the highest rank; all the others, who were more or less pretty, were favourites of the prince, all his days a great lover of the fair sex. Two of these ladies danced the Forlana, and the Elector was much amused in making me dance it also. I have already said that the Forlana is a Venetian dance, and one of the most energetic kind imaginable. It is danced by a lady and gentleman opposite to one another, and as the two ladies relieved one another they were almost the death of me. One has to be strong to dance twelve turns, and after the thirteenth I felt I could do no more, and begged for mercy.

Soon after we danced another dance, where each gentleman kisses a lady. I was not too shy, and each time I continued to kiss my mistress with considerable ardour, which made the peasant-elector burst with laughter and the peasant-general burst with rage.

In a lull between the dances, this charming and original woman found means to tell me in private that all the Cologne ladies would leave at noon on the next day, and that I would increase my popularity by inviting them all to breakfast at Bruhl.

"Send each one a note with the name of her cavalier, and trust in Count Verita to do everything for the best; you need only tell him that you wish to give an entertainment similar to that given two years ago by the Prince de Deux-Ponts. Lose no time. You will have a score of guests; mind you let them know the hour of the repast. Take care, too, that your invitations are sent round by nine o'clock in the morning."

All these instructions were uttered with lightning speed, and I, enchanted with the power my mistress thought she possessed over me, thought only of obeying, without reflecting whether I owed her obedience. Bruhl, breakfast, a score of people like the Prince Deux-

Ponts, invitations to the ladies, Count Verita; I knew as much as she could have told me if she had taken an hour.

I left the room in my peasant's dress, and begged a page to take me to Count Verita, who began to laugh on seeing my attire. I told my business with the importance of an ambassador, and this made him in a still better humour.

"It can all easily be arranged," said he, "I have only to write to the steward, and I will do so immediately. But how much do you want to spend?"

"As much as possible."

"As little as possible, I suppose you mean."

"Not at all; I want to treat my guests with magnificence."

"All the same you must fix on a sum, as I know whom I've got to deal with."

"Well, well! two-three hundred ducats; will that do?"

"Two hundred; the Prince de Deux-Ponts did not spend more."

He began to write, and gave me his word that everything should be in readiness. I left him and addressing myself to a sharp Italian page said that I would give two ducats to the valet who would furnish me with the names of the Cologne ladies who were in Bonn, and of the gentlemen who had accompanied them. I got what I wanted in less than half an hour, and before leaving the ball I told my mistress that all should be done according to her desires.

I wrote eighteen notes before I went to bed, and in the morning a confidential servant had delivered them before nine o'clock.

At nine o'clock I went to take leave of Count Verita, who gave me, on behalf of the Elector, a superb gold snuff-box with his portrait set in diamonds. I was very sensible of this mark of kindness, and I wished to go and thank his serene highness before my departure, but my friendly fellow-countryman told me that I might put off doing so till I passed through Bonn on my way to Frankfort.

Breakfast was ordered for one o'clock. At noon I had arrived at Bruhl, a country house of the Elector's, with nothing remarkable about it save its furniture. In this it is a poor copy of the Trianon. In a fine hall I found a table laid for twenty-four persons, arranged with silver gilt plates, damask linen, and exquisite china, while the sideboard was adorned with an immense quantity of silver and silvergilt plate. At one end of the room were two other tables laden with sweets and the choicest wines procurable. I announced myself as the host, and the cook told me I should be perfectly satisfied.

"The collation," said he, "will be composed of only twenty-four dishes, but in addition there will be twenty-four dishes of English oysters and a splendid dessert."

I saw a great number of servants, and told him that they would not be necessary, but he said they were, as the guests' servants could not be admitted.

I received all my guests at the door, confining my compliments to begging their pardons for having been so bold as to procure myself this great honour.

The breakfast was served at one exactly, and I had the pleasure of enjoying the astonishment in my mistress's eyes when she saw that I had treated them as well as a prince of the empire. She was aware that everybody knew her to be the chief object of this lavish outlay, but she was delighted to see that I did not pay her any attentions which were at all invidious. The table was seated for twenty-four, and though I had only asked eighteen people every place was occupied. Three couples, therefore, had come without being asked; but that pleased me all the more. Like a courtly cavalier I would not sit down, but waited on the ladies, going from one to the other, eating the dainty bits they gave me, and seeing that all had what they wanted.

By the time the oysters were done twenty bottles of champagne had been emptied, so that when the actual breakfast commenced everybody began to talk at once. The meal might easily have passed for a splendid dinner, and I was glad to see that not a drop of water was drunk, for the Champagne, Tokay, Rhine wine, Madeira, Malaga, Cyprus, Alicante, and Cape wine would not allow it.

Before dessert was brought on an enormous dish of truffles was placed on the table. I advised my guests to take Maraschino with it, and those ladies who appreciated the liqueur drank it as if it had been water. The dessert was really sumptuous. In it were displayed the portraits of all the monarchs of Europe. Everyone complimented the cook on his achievement, and he, his vanity being tickled and wishing to appear good-natured, said that none of it would spoil in the pocket, and accordingly everybody took as much as they chose.

General Kettler, who, in spite of his jealousy and the part he saw me play, had no suspicion of the real origin of the banquet, said,

"I will wager that this is the Elector's doing. His highness has desired to preserve his incognito, and M. Casanova has played his part to admiration."

This remark set all the company in a roar.

"General," said I, "if the Elector had given me such an order, I should, of course, have obeyed him, but I should have felt it a humiliating part to play. His highness, however, has deigned to do me a far greater honour; look here." So saying, I shewed him the gold snuff-box, which made the tour of the table two or three times over.

When we had finished, we rose from table, astonished to find we had been engaged for three hours in a pleasurable occupation, which all would willingly have prolonged; but at last we had to part, and after many compliments they all went upon their way, in order to be in time for the theatre. As well pleased as my guests,

I left twenty ducats with the steward, for the servants, and promised him to let Count Verita know of my satisfaction in writing.

I arrived at Cologne in time for the French play, and as I had no carriage I went to the theatre in a sedan chair. As soon as I got into the house, I saw the Comte de Lastic alone with my fair one. I thought this a good omen, and I went to them directly. As soon as she saw me, she said with a melancholy air that the general had got so ill that he had been obliged to go to bed. Soon after, M. de Lastic left us, and dropping her assumed melancholy she made me, with the utmost grace, a thousand compliments, which compensated me for the expenses of my breakfast a hundred times over.

"The general," said she, "had too much to drink; he is an envious devil, and has discovered that it is not seemly of you to treat us as if you were a prince. I told him that, on the contrary, you had treated us as if we were princes, waiting on us with your napkin on your arm. He thereupon found fault with me for degrading you."

"Why do you not send him about his business? So rude a fellow is not worthy of serving so famous a beauty."

"It's too late. A woman whom you don't know would get possession of him.
I should be obliged to conceal my feelings, and that would vex me."

"I understand—I understand. Would that I were a great prince! In the mean time, let me tell you that my sickness is greater than Kettler's."

"You are joking, I hope."

"Nay, not at all; I am speaking seriously, for the kisses I was so happy to snatch from you at the ball have inflamed my blood, and if you have not enough kindness to cure me in the only possible way I shall leave Cologne with a life-long grief."

"Put off your departure: why should you desire to go to Stuttgart so earnestly? I think of you, believe me, and I do not wish to deceive you; but it is hard to find an opportunity."

"If you had not the general's carriage waiting for you to-night, and I had mine, I could take you home with perfect propriety."

"Hush! As you have not your carriage, it is my part to take you home. It is a splendid idea, that we must so contrive it that it may not seem to be a concerted plan. You must give me your arm to my carriage, and I shall then ask you where your carriage is; you will answer that you have not got one. I shall ask you to come into mine, and I will drop you at your hotel. It will only give us a couple of minutes, but that is something till we are more fortunate."

I replied to her only by a look which expressed the intoxication of my spirits at the prospect of so great bliss.

Although the play was quite a short one, it seemed to me to last for ever. At last the curtain fell, and we went downstairs. When we got to the portico she asked me the questions we had agreed upon, and when I told her I had not got a carriage, she said, "I am going to the general's to ask after his health; if it will not take you too much out of your way, I can leave you at your lodging as we come back."

It was a grand idea. We should pass the entire length of the ill-paved town twice, and thus we secured a little more time. Unfortunately, the carriage was a chariot, and as we were going the moon shone directly on us. On that occasion the planet was certainly not entitled to the appellation of the lovers' friend. We did all we could, but that was almost nothing, and I found the attempt a desperate one, though my lovely partner endeavoured to help me as much as possible. To add to our discomforts, the inquisitive and impudent coachman kept turning his head round, which forced us to moderate the energy of our movements. The sentry at the general's door told our coachman that his excellency could see no one, and we joyfully turned towards my hotel, and now that the moon was behind us and the man's curiosity less inconvenient, we got on a little better, or rather not so badly as before, but the horses seemed to me to fly rather than gallop; however, feeling that it would be well to have the coachman on my side in case of another opportunity, I gave him a ducat as I got down.

I entered the hotel feeling vexed and unhappy, though more in love than ever, for my fair one had convinced me that she was no passive mistress, but could experience pleasure as well as give it. That being the case I resolved not to leave Cologne before we had drained the cup of pleasure together, and that, it seemed to me, could not take place till the general was out of the way.

Next day, at noon, I went to the general's house to write down my name, but I found he was receiving visitors and I went in. I made the general an appropriate compliment, to which the rude Austrian only replied by a cold inclination of the head. He was surrounded by a good many officers, and after four minutes I made a general bow and went out. The boor kept his room for three days, and as my mistress did not come to the theatre I had not the pleasure of seeing her.

On the last day of the carnival Kettler asked a good many people to a ball and supper. On my going to pay my court to my mistress in her box at the theatre, and being left for a moment alone with her, she asked me if I were invited to the general's supper. I answered in the negative.

"What!" said she, in an imperious and indignant voice, "he has not asked you? You must go, for all that."

"Consider what you say," said I, gently, "I will do anything to please you but that."

"I know all you can urge; nevertheless, you must go. I should feel insulted if you were not at that supper. If you love me you will give me this proof of your affection and (I think I may say) esteem."

"You ask me thus? Then I will go. But are you aware that you are exposing me to the danger of losing my life or taking his? for I am not the man to pass over an affront."

"I know all you can say," said she. "I have your honour at heart as much as mine, or perhaps more so, but nothing will happen to you; I will answer for everything. You must go, and you must give me your promise now, for I am resolved if you do not go, neither will I, but we must never see each other more."

"Then you may reckon upon me."

At that moment M. de Castries came in, and I left the box and went to the pit, where I passed two anxious hours in reflecting on the possible consequences of the strange step this woman would have me take. Nevertheless, such was the sway of her beauty over my soul, I determined to abide by my promise and to carry the matter through, and to put myself in the wrong as little as possible. I went to the general's at the end of the play, and only found five or six people there. I went up to a canoness who was very fond of Italian poetry, and had no trouble in engaging her in an interesting discussion. In half an hour the room was full, my mistress coming in last on the general's arm. I was taken up with the canoness and did not stir, and consequently Kettler did not notice me, while the lady in great delight at seeing me left him no time to examine his guests, and he was soon talking to some people at the other end of the room. In a quarter of an hour afterwards supper was announced. The canoness rose, took my arm, and we seated ourselves at table together, still talking about Italian literature. Then came the catastrophe. When all the places had been taken one gentleman was left standing, there being no place for him. "How can that have happened?" said the general, raising his voice, and while the servants were bringing another chair and arranging another place he passed his guests in review. All the while I pretended not to notice what was going on, but when he came to me he said loudly,

"Sir, I did not ask you to come."

"That is quite true, general," I said, respectfully, "but I thought, no doubt correctly, that the omission was due to forgetfulness, and I thought myself obliged all the same to come and pay my court to your excellency."

Without a pause I renewed my conversation with the canoness, not so much as looking around. A dreadful silence reigned for four or five minutes, but the canoness began to utter witticisms which I took up and communicated to my neighbours, so that in a short time the whole table was in good spirits except the general, who preserved a sulky silence. This did not much matter to me, but my vanity was concerned in smoothing him down, and I watched for my opportunity.

M. de Castries was praising the dauphin, and his brothers, the Comte de Lusace and the Duc de Courlande, were mentioned; this led the conversation up to Prince Biron, formerly a duke, who was in Siberia, and his personal qualities were discussed, one of the guests having said that his chiefest merit was to have pleased the Empress Anne. I begged his pardon, saying,—

"His greatest merit was to have served faithfully the last Duke Kettler; who if it had not been for the courage of him who is now so unfortunate, would have lost all his belongings in the war. It was Duke Kettler who so heroically sent him to the Court of St. Petersburg, but Biron never asked for the duchy. An earldom would have satisfied him, as he recognized the rights of the younger branch of the Kettler family, which would be reigning now if it were not for the empress's whim: nothing would satisfy her but to confer a dukedom on the favourite."

The general, whose face had cleared while I was speaking, said, in the most polite manner of which he was capable, that I was a person of remarkable information, adding regretfully,—

"Yes, if it were not for that whim I should be reigning now."

After this modest remark he burst into a fit of laughter and sent me down a bottle of the best Rhine wine, and addressed his conversation to me till the supper was over. I quietly enjoyed the turn things had taken, but still more the pleasure I saw expressed in the beautiful eyes of my mistress.

Dancing went on all night, and I did not leave my canoness, who was a delightful woman and danced admirably. With my lady I only danced one minuet. Towards the end of the ball the general, to finish up with a piece of awkwardness, asked me if I was going soon. I replied that I did not think of leaving Cologne till after the grand review.

I went to bed full of joy at having given the burgomaster's wife such a signal proof of my love, and full of gratitude to fortune

---

who had helped me so in dealing with my doltish general, for God knows what I should have done if he had forgotten himself so far as to tell me to leave the table! The next time I saw the fair she told me she had felt a mortal pang of fear shoot through her when the general said he had not asked me.

"I am quite sure," said she, "that he would have gone further, if your grand answer had not stopped his mouth; but if he had said another word, my mind was made up."

"To do what?"

"I should have risen from the table and taken your arm, and we should have gone out together. M. de Castries has told me that he would have done the same, and I believe all the ladies whom you asked to breakfast would have followed our example."

"But the affair would not have stopped then, for I should certainly have demanded immediate satisfaction, and if he had refused it I should have struck him with the flat of my sword."

"I know that, but pray forget that it was I who exposed you to this danger. For my part, I shall never forget what I owe to you, and I will try to convince you of my gratitude."

Two days later, on hearing that she was indisposed, I went to call on her at eleven o'clock, at which time I was sure the general would not be there. She received me in her husband's room, and he, in the friendliest manner possible, asked me if I had come to dine with them. I hastened to thank him for his invitation, which I accepted with pleasure, and I enjoyed this dinner better than Kettler's supper. The burgomaster was a fine-looking man, pleasant-mannered and intelligent, and a lover of peace and quietness. His wife, whom he adored, ought to have loved him, since he was by no means one of those husbands whose motto is, "Displease whom you like, so long as you please me."

On her husband's going out for a short time, she shewed me over the house.

"Here is our bedroom," said she; "and this is the closet in which I sleep for five or six nights in every month. Here is a church which we may look upon as our private chapel, as we hear mass from those two grated windows. On Sundays we go down this stair and enter the church by a door, the key to which is always in my keeping." It was the second Saturday in Lent; we had an excellent fasting dinner, but I did not for once pay much attention to eating. To see this young and beautiful woman surrounded by her children, adored by her family, seemed to me a beautiful sight. I left them at an early hour to write to Esther, whom I did not neglect, all occupied as I was with this new flame.

Next day I went to hear mass at the little church next to the burgomaster's house. I was well cloaked so as not to attract attention. I saw my fair one going out wearing a capuchin, and followed by her family. I noted the little door which was so recessed in the wall that it would have escaped the notice of anyone who was unaware of its existence; it opened, I saw, towards the staircase.

The devil, who, as everybody knows, has more power in a church than anywhere else, put into my head the idea of enjoying my mistress by means of the door and stair. I told her my plan the next day at the theatre.

"I have thought of it as well as you," said she, laughing, "and I will give you the necessary instructions in writing; you will find them in the first gazette I send you."

We could not continue this pleasant interview, as my mistress had with her a lady from Aix-la-Chapelle, who was staying with her for a few days. And indeed the box was full of company.

I had not long to wait, for next day she gave me back the gazette openly, telling me that she had not found anything to interest her in it. I knew that it would be exceedingly interesting to me. Her note was as follows:

"The design which love inspired is subject not to difficulty but uncertainty. The wife only sleeps in the closet when her husband asks her—an event which only occurs at certain periods, and the separation does not last for more than a few days. This period is not far off, but long custom has made it impossible for the wife to impose on her husband. It will, therefore, be necessary to wait. Love will warn you when the hour of bliss has come. The plan will be to hide in the church; and there must be no thought of seducing the door-keeper, for though poor he is too stupid to be bribed, and would betray the secret. The only way will be to hide so as to elude his watchfulness. He shuts the church at noon on working days; on feast days he shuts it at evening, and he always opens it again at dawn. When the time comes, all that need be done is to give the door a gentle push-it will not be locked. As the closet which is to be the scene of the blissful combat is only separated from the room by a partition, there must be no spitting, coughing, nor nose-blowing: it would be fatal. The escape will be a matter of no difficulty; one can go down to the church, and go out as soon as it is opened. Since the beadle has seen nobody in the evening, it is not likely that he will see more in the morning."

I kissed again and again this charming letter, which I thought shewed great power of mental combination, and I went next day to see how the coast lay: this was the first thing to be done. There was a chair in the church in which I should never have been seen, but the stair was on the sacristy side, and that was always locked up. I decided on occupying the confessional, which was close to the door. I could creep into the space beneath the confessor's seat, but it was so small that I doubted my ability to stay there after the door was shut. I waited till noon to make the attempt, and as soon as the church was empty I took up my position. I had to roll myself up into a ball, and even then I was so badly concealed by the folding door that anyone happening to pass by at two paces distance might easily have seen me. However I did not care for that, for in adventures of that nature one must leave a great deal to fortune. Determined to run all risks I went home highly pleased with my observations. I put everything I had determined down in writing, and sent it to her box at the theatre, enclosed in an old gazette.

A week after she asked the general in my presence if her husband could do anything for him at Aix-la-Chapelle, where he was going on the morrow, with the intention of returning in three days. That was enough for me, but a glance from her added meaning to her words. I was all the more glad as I had a slight cold, and the next day being a feast day I could take up my position at night fall, and thus avoid a painful vigil of several hours' duration.

I curled myself up in the confessional at four o'clock, hiding myself as best I could, and commending myself to the care of all the saints. At five o'clock the beadle made his usual tour of inspection, went out and locked the door. As soon as I heard the noise of the key I came out of my narrow cell and sat down on a bench facing the windows. Soon after my mistress's shadow appeared on the grated panes, and I knew she had seen me.

I sat on the bench for a quarter of an hour and then pushed open the little door and entered. I shut it and sat down on the lowest step of the stair, and spent there five hours which would probably have not been unpleasant ones if I had not been dreadfully tormented by the rats running to and fro close to me. Nature has given me a great dislike to this animal, which is comparatively harmless; but the smell of rats always sickens me.

At last I heard the clock strike ten, the hour of bliss, and I saw the form of my beloved holding a candle, and I was then freed from my painful position. If my readers have been in such a situation they can imagine the pleasures of that happy night, but they cannot divine the minute circumstances; for if I was an expert my partner had an inexhaustible store of contrivances for augmenting the bliss of that sweet employment. She had taken care to get me a little collation, which looked delicious, but which I could not touch, my appetite lying in another quarter.

For seven hours, which I thought all too short, we enjoyed one another, not resting, except for talk, which served to heighten our pleasure.

The burgomaster was not the man for an ardent passion, but his strength of constitution enabled him to do his duty to his wife every night without failing, but, whether from regard to his health or from a religious scruple, he suspended his rights every month while the moon exercised hers, and to put himself out of temptation he made his wife sleep apart. But for once in a way, the lady was not in the position of a divorcee.

Exhausted, but not satiated with pleasure, I left her at day-break, assuring her that when we met again she would find me the same; and with that I went to hide in the confessional, fearing lest the growing light might betray me to the beadle. However, I got away without any difficulty, and passed nearly the whole day in bed, having my dinner served to me in my room. In the evening I went to the theatre, to have the pleasure of seeing the beloved object of whom my love and constancy had made me the possessor.

At the end of a fortnight she sent me a note in which she told me that she would sleep by herself on the night following. It was a ferial day, and I therefore went to the church at eleven in the morning after making an enormous breakfast. I hid myself as before, and the beadle locked me in without making any discovery.

I had a wait of ten hours, and the reflection that I should have to spend the time partly in the church and partly on the dark and rat-haunted staircase, without being able to take a pinch of snuff for fear of being obliged to blow my nose, did not tend to enliven the prospect; however, the hope of the great reward made it easy to be borne. But at one o'clock I heard a slight noise, and looking up saw a hand appear through the grated window, and a paper drop on the floor of the church. I ran to pick it up, while my heart beat fast, for my first idea was that some obstacle had occurred which would compel me to pass the night on a bench in the church. I opened it, and what was my joy to read as follows:

"The door is open, and you will be more comfortable on the staircase, where you will find a light, a little dinner, and some books, than in the church. The seat is not very easy, but I have done my best to remedy the discomfort with a cushion. Trust me, the time will seem as long to me as to you, but be patient. I have told the general that I do not feel very well, and shall not go out to-day. May God keep you from coughing, especially during the night, for on the least noise we should be undone."

What stratagems are inspired by love! I opened the door directly, and found a nicely-laid meal, dainty viands, delicious wine, coffee, a chafing dish, lemons, spirits of wine, sugar, and rum to make some punch if I liked. With these comforts and some books, I could wait well enough; but I was astonished at the dexterity of my charming mistress in doing all this without the knowledge of anybody in the house.

I spent three hours in reading, and three more in eating, and making coffee and punch, and then I went to sleep. At ten o'clock my darling came and awoke me. This second night was delicious, but not so much so as the former, as we could not see each other, and the violence of our ecstatic combats was restrained by the vicinity of the good husband. We slept part of the time, and early in the morning I had to make good my retreat. Thus ended my amour with this lady. The general went to Westphalia, and she was soon to go into the country. I thus made my preparations for leaving Cologne, promising to come and see her the year following, which promise however I was precluded, as the reader will see, from keeping. I took leave of my acquaintance and set out, regretted by all.

The stay of two months and a half which I made in Cologne did not diminish my monetary resources, although I lost whenever I was persuaded to play. However, my winnings at Bonn made up all deficiencies, and my banker, M. Franck, complained that I had not made any use of him. However, I was obliged to be prudent so that those persons who spied into my actions might find nothing reprehensible.

I left Cologne about the middle of March, and I stopped at Bonn, to present my respects to the Elector, but he was away. I dined with Count Verita and the Abbe Scampar, a favourite of the Elector's. After dinner the count gave me a letter of introduction to a canoness at Coblentz, of whom he spoke in very high terms. That obliged me to stop at Coblentz; but when I got down at the inn, I found that the canoness was at Manheim, while in her stead I encountered an actress named Toscani, who was going to

Stuttgart with her young and pretty daughter. She was on her way from Paris, where her daughter had been learning character-dancing with the famous Vestris. I had known her at Paris, but had not seen much of her, though I had given her a little spaniel dog, which was the joy of her daughter. This daughter was a perfect jewel, who had very little difficulty in persuading me to come with them to Stuttgart, where I expected, for other reasons, to have a very pleasant stay. The mother was impatient to know what the duke would think of her daughter, for she had destined her from her childhood to serve the pleasures of this voluptuous prince, who, though he had a titular mistress, was fond of experimenting with all the ballet-girls who took his fancy.

We made up a little supper-party, and it may be guessed that two of us belonging to the boards the conversation was not exactly a course in moral theology. The Toscani told me that her daughter was a neophyte, and that she had made up her mind not to let the duke touch her till he had dismissed his reigning mistress, whose place she was designed to take. The mistress in question was a dancer named Gardella, daughter of a Venetian boatman, whose name has been mentioned in my first volume—in fine, she was the wife of Michel d'Agata, whom I found at Munich fleeing from the terrible Leads, where I myself languished for so long.

As I seemed to doubt the mother's assertion, and threw out some rather broad hints to the effect that I believed that the first bloom had been plucked at Paris, and that the Duke of Wurtemburg would only have the second, their vanity was touched; and on my proposing to verify the matter with my own eyes it was solemnly agreed that this ceremony should take place the next day. They kept their promise, and I was pleasantly engaged for two hours the next morning, and was at last obliged to extinguish in the mother the flames her daughter had kindled in my breast.

Although the Toscani was young enough, she would have found me ice if her daughter had been able to satisfy my desires, but she did not trust me well enough to leave us alone together. As it was she was well satisfied.

I resolved, then, on going to Stuttgart in company with the two nymphs, and I expected to see there the Binetti, who was always an enthusiastic admirer of mine. This actress was the daughter of a Roman boatman. I had helped her to get on the boards the same year that Madame de Valmarana had married her to a French dancer named Binet, whose name she had Italianized by the addition of one syllable, like those who ennoble themselves by adding another syllable to their names. I also expected to see the Gardella, young Baletti, of whom I was very fond, his young wife the Vulcani, and several other of my old friends, who I thought would combine to make my stay at Stuttgart a very pleasant one. But it will be seen that it is a risky thing to reckon without one's host. At the last posting station I bid adieu to my two friends, and went to the "Bear."

CHAPTER XII

Gardella Portrait of The Duke of Wurtemburg—My Dinner with Gardella, And its Consequences—Unfortunate Meeting I Play and Lose Four Thousand Louis—Lawsuit—Lucky Flight—My Arrival at Zurich—Church Consecrated By Jesus Christ Himself

At that period the Court of the Duke of Wurtemburg was the most brilliant in Europe. The heavy subsidies paid by France for quartering ten thousand men upon him furnished him with the means for indulging in luxury and debauchery. The army in question was a fine body of men, but during the war it was distinguished only by its blunders.

The duke was sumptuous in his tastes, which were for splendid palaces, hunting establishments on a large scale, enormous stables—in short, every whim imaginable; but his chief expense was the large salaries he paid his theatre, and, above all, his mistresses. He had a French play, an Italian opera, grand and comic, and twenty Italian dancers, all of whom had been principal dancers in Italian theatres. His director of ballets was Novers, and sometimes five hundred dancers appeared at once. A clever machinist and the best scene painters did their best to make the audience believe in magic. All the ballet-girls were pretty, and all of them boasted of having been enjoyed at least once by my lord. The chief of them was a Venetian, daughter of a gondolier named Gardella. She was brought up by the senator Malipiero, whom my readers know for his good offices towards myself, who had her taught for the theatre, and gave her a dancing-master. I found her at Munich, after my flight from The Leads, married to Michel

Agata. The duke took a fancy to her, and asked her husband, who was only too happy to agree, to yield her; but he was satisfied with her charms in a year, and put her on the retired list with the title of madame.

This honour had made all the other ballet-girls jealous, and they all thought themselves as fit as she to be taken to the duke's titular mistress, especially as she only enjoyed the honour without the pleasure. They all intrigued to procure her dismissal, but the Venetian lady succeeded in holding her ground against all cabals.

Far from reproaching the duke for this incorrigible infidelity, she encouraged him in it, and was very glad to be left to herself, as she cared nothing for him. Her chief pleasure was to have the ballet-girls who aspired to the honours of the handkerchief come to her to solicit her good offices. She always received them politely, gave them her advice, and bade them do their best to please the prince. In his turn the duke thought himself bound to shew his gratitude for her good nature, and gave her in public all the honours which could be given to a princess.

I was not long in finding out that the duke's chief desire was to be talked about. He would have liked people to say that there was not a prince in Europe to compare with him for wit, taste, genius, in the invention of pleasures, and statesman-like capacities; he would fain be regarded as a Hercules in the pleasures of Bacchus and Venus, and none the less an Aristides in governing his people. He dismissed without pity an attendant who failed to wake him after he had been forced to yield to sleep for three or four hours, but he did not care how roughly he was awakened.

It has happened that after having given his highness a large cup of coffee, the servant has been obliged to throw him into a bath of cold water, where the duke had to choose between awaking or drowning.

As soon as he was dressed the duke would assemble his council and dispatch whatever business was on hand, and then he would give audience to whoever cared to come into his presence. Nothing could be more comic than the audiences he gave to his poorer subjects. Often there came to him dull peasants and workmen of the lowest class; the poor duke would sweat and rage to make them hear reason, in which he was sometimes unsuccessful, and his petitioners would go away terrified, desperate, and furious. As to the pretty country maidens, he examined into their complaints in private, and though he seldom did anything for them they went away consoled.

The subsidies which the French Crown was foolish enough to pay him for a perfectly useless service did not suffice for his extravagant expenses. He loaded his subjects with taxes till the patient people could bear it no longer, and some years after had recourse to the Diet of Wetzlar, which obliged him to change his system. He was foolish enough to wish to imitate the King of Prussia, while that monarch made fun of the duke, and called him his ape. His wife was the daughter of the Margrave of Bayreuth, the prettiest and most accomplished princess in all Germany. When I had come to Stuttgart she was no longer there;

she had taken refuge with her father, on account of a disgraceful affront which had been offered her by her unworthy husband. It is incorrect to say that this princess fled from her husband because of his infidelities.

After I had dined by myself, I dressed and went to the opera provided gratis by the duke in the fine theatre he had built. The prince was in the front of the orchestra, surrounded by his brilliant Court. I sat in a box on the first tier, delighted to be able to hear so well the music of the famous Jumella, who was in the duke's service. In my ignorance of the etiquette of small German Courts I happened to applaud a solo, which had been exquisitely sung by a castrato whose name I have forgotten, and directly afterwards an individual came into my box and addressed me in a rude manner. However, I knew no German, and could only answer by 'nich verstand'—"I don't understand."

He went out, and soon after an official came in, who told me, in good
French, that when the sovereign was present all applause was forbidden.

"Very good, sir. Then I will go away and come again when the sovereign is not here, as when an air pleases me I always applaud."

After this reply I called for my carriage, but just as I was getting into it the same official came and told me that the duke wanted to speak to me. I accordingly followed him to the presence.

"You are M. Casanova, are you?" said the duke.

"Yes, my lord."

"Where do you come from?"

"From Cologne."

"Is this the first time you have been to Stuttgart?"

"Yes, my lord."

"Do you think of staying long?"

"For five or six days, if your highness will allow me."

"Certainly, you may stay as long as you like, and you may clap when you please."

"I shall profit by your permission, my lord."

"Good."

I sat down again, and the whole audience settled down to the play. Soon after, an actor sung an air which the duke applauded, and of course all the courtiers, but not caring much for the song I sat still—everyone to his taste. After the ballet the duke went to the favourite's box, kissed her hand, and left the theatre. An official, who was sitting by me and did not know that I was acquainted with the Gardella, told me that as I had had the honour of speaking to the prince I might obtain the honour of kissing his favourite's hand.

I felt a strong inclination to laugh, but I restrained myself; and a sudden and very irrational impulse made me say that she was a relation of mine. The words had no sooner escaped me than I bit my lip, for this stupid lie could only do me harm, but it was decreed that I should do nothing at Stuttgart but commit blunders. The officer, who seemed astonished at my reply, bowed and went to the favourite's box to inform her of my presence. The Gardelia looked in my direction and beckoned to me with her fan, and I hastened to comply with the invitation, laughing inwardly at the part I was going to play. As soon as I came in she graciously gave me her hand, which I kissed, calling her my cousin.

"Did you tell the duke you were my cousin?" said she.

"No," I replied.

"Very good, then I will do so myself; come and dine with me to-morrow."

She then left the house, and I went to visit the ballet-girls, who were undressing: The Binetti, who was one of the oldest of my acquaintances, was in an ecstasy of joy at seeing me, and asked me to dine with her every day. Cartz, the violin, who had been with me in the orchestra at St. Samuel's, introduced me to his pretty daughter, saying,

"She is not made for the duke's eyes to gaze on, and he shall never have her."

The good man was no prophet, as the duke got possession of her a short time after. She presented him with two babies, but these pledges of affection could not fix the inconstant prince.

Nevertheless, she was a girl of the most captivating kind, for to the most perfect beauty she added grace, wit, goodness, and kindness, which won everyone's heart. But the duke was satiated, and his only pleasure lay in novelty.

After her I saw the Vulcani, whom I had known at Dresden, and who suddenly presented her husband to me. He threw his arms round my neck. He was Baletti, brother of my faithless one, a young man of great talent of whom I was very fond.

I was surrounded by all these friends, when the officer whom I had so foolishly told that I was related to the Gardella came in and began to tell the story. The Binetti, after hearing it, said to him,

"It's a lie."

"But my dear," said I to her, "you can't be better informed on the subject than I am." She replied by laughing, but Cartz said, very wittily,

"As Gardella is only a boatman's daughter, like Binetti, the latter thinks, and very rightly, that you ought to have given her the refusal of your cousinship."

Next day I had a pleasant dinner with the favourite, though she told me that, not having seen the duke, she could not tell me how he would take my pleasantry, which her mother resented very much. This mother of hers, a woman of the lowest birth, had become very proud since her daughter was a prince's mistress, and thought my relationship a blot on their escutcheon. She had the impudence to tell me that her relations had never been players, without reflecting that it must be worse to descend to this estate than to rise from it, if it were dishonourable. I ought to have pitied her, but not being of a forbearing nature I retorted by asking if her sister was still alive, a question which made her frown and to which she gave no answer. The sister I spoke of was a fat blind woman, who begged on a bridge in Venice.

After having spent a pleasant day with the favourite, who was the oldest of my theatrical friends, I left her, promising to come to breakfast the next day; but as I was going out the porter bade me not to put my feet there again, but would not say on whose authority he gave me this polite order. It would have been wiser to hold my tongue, as this stroke must have come from the mother; or, perhaps, from the daughter, whose vanity I had wounded: she was a good-enough actress to conceal her anger.

I was angry with myself, and went away in an ill humour; I was humiliated to see myself treated in such a manner by a wretched wanton of an actress; though if I had been more discreet I could have got a welcome in the best society. If I had not promised to dine with Binetti the next day I should have posted off forthwith, and I should thus have escaped all the misadventures which befell me in that wretched town.

The Binetti lived in the house of her lover, the Austrian ambassador, and the part of the house she occupied adjoined the town wall. As will be seen; this detail is an important one. I dined alone with my good fellow-countrywoman, and if I had felt myself capable of love at that period all my old affection would have resumed its sway over me, as her beauty was undiminished, and she had more tact and knowledge of the world than when I knew her formerly.

The Austrian ambassador was a good-natured, easygoing, and generous man; as for her husband he was not worthy of her, and she never saw him. I spent a pleasant day with her, talking of our old friends, and as I had nothing to keep me in Wurtemburg I decided to leave in two days, as I had promised the Toscani and her daughter to go with them on the next day to Louisbourg. We were to start at five in the morning, but the following adventure befell me:—

As I was leaving Binetti's house I was greeted very courteously by three officers whom I had become acquainted with at the coffee house, and I walked along the promenade with them.

"We are going," said one of them, "to visit certain ladies of easy virtue; we shall be glad to have you of our company."

"I only speak a few words of German," I answered, "and if I join you I shall be bored."

"Ah! but the ladies are Italians," they exclaimed, "nothing could suit you better."

I did not at all like following them, but my evil genius led me in that wretched town from one blunder to another, and so I went in spite of myself.

We turned back into the town, and I let myself be led up to the third floor of an ill-looking house, and in the meanest of rooms I saw the pretended nieces of Peccini. A moment after Peccini appeared, and had the impudence to throw his arms around my neck, calling me his best friend. His nieces overwhelmed me with caresses, and seemed to confirm the idea that we were old friends. I did nothing and held my tongue.

The officers prepared for a debauch; I did not imitate their example, but this made no difference to them. I saw into what an evil place I had been decoyed, but a false shame prevented me from leaving the house without ceremony. I was wrong, but I determined to be more prudent for the future.

Before long a pot-house supper was served, of which I did not partake; but not wishing to seem bad company I drank two or three small glasses of Hungarian wine. After supper, which did not last very long, cards were produced, and one of the officers held a bank at faro. I punted and lost the fifty or sixty Louis I had about me. I felt that I was drunk, my head was reeling, and I would have gladly given over playing and gone away, but I have never been so possessed as on that day, either from false shame or from the effects of the drugged wine they gave me. My noble officers seemed vexed that I had lost, and would give me my revenge. They made me hold a bank of a hundred Louis in fish, which they counted out to me. I did so, and lost. I made a bank again, and again I lost. My inflamed understanding, my increasing drunkenness, and my anger, deprived me of all sense, and I kept increasing my bank, losing all the time, till at midnight my good rascals declared they would play no more. They made a calculation, and declared that I had lost nearly a hundred thousand francs. So great was my intoxication, although I had had no more wine, that they were obliged to send for a sedan chair to take me to my inn. While my servant was undressing me he discovered that I had neither my watches nor my gold snuff-boy.

"Don't forget to wake me at four in the morning," said I. Therewith I went to bed and enjoyed a calm and refreshing sleep.

While I was dressing next morning I found a hundred Louis in my pocket, at which I was much astonished, for my dizziness of brain being over now, I remembered that I had not this money about me the evening before; but my mind was taken up with the pleasure party, and I put off thinking of this incident and of my enormous losses till afterwards. I went to the Toscani and we set out for Louisbourg, where we had a capital dinner, and my spirits ran so high that my companions could never have guessed the misfortune that had just befallen me. We went back to Stuttgart in the evening.

When I got home my Spaniard told me that they knew nothing about my watches and snuff-box at the house where I had been the evening before, and that the three officers had come to call on me, but not finding me at home they had told him to warn me that they would breakfast with me on the following morning. They kept the appointment.

"Gentlemen," said I, as soon as they came in, "I have lost a sum which I cannot pay, and which I certainly should not have lost without the drugged wine you gave me. You have taken me to a den of infamy, where I was shamefully robbed of jewellery to the value of more than three hundred Louis. I complain of no one, since I have only my own folly to complain of. If I had been wiser all this would not have happened to me."

They exclaimed loudly at this speech, and tried to play the part of men of honour. They spoke in vain, as I had made up my mind to pay nothing.

Whilst we were in the thick of the fight, and were beginning to get angry over it, Baletti, Toscani, and Binetti came in, and heard the discussion. I then had breakfast brought in, and after we had finished my friends left me.

When we were once more alone, one of the rascals addressed me as follows:

"We are too honest, sir, to take advantage of your position. You have been unfortunate, but all men are sometimes unfortunate, and we ask nothing better than a mutual accommodation. We will take over all your properties; jewels, diamonds, arms, and carriage, and have them valued; and if the sum realized does not cover your debt we will take your acceptance, payable at date, and remain good friends."

"Sir, I do not wish for the friendship of robbers, and I will not play a single farthing."

At this they tried threats, but I kept cool and said,—

"Gentlemen, your menaces will not intimidate me, and, as far as I can see, you have only two ways of getting paid; either by way of the law, in which case I do not think I shall find it difficult to get a barrister to take up my case, or, secondly, you can pay yourselves on my body, honourably, with sword in hand."

As I had expected, they replied that if I wished they would do me the honour of killing me after I had paid them. They went off cursing, telling me that I would be sorry for what I had said.

Soon after I went out and spent the day with the Toscani in gaiety which, situated as I was, was not far off madness. At the time I placed it to the daughter's charms, and to the need my spirits were in of recovering their elasticity.

However, the mother having witnessed the rage of the three robbers was the first to urge me to fortify myself against their villainy by an appeal to the law.

"If you give them the start," said she, "they may possibly gain a great advantage over you in spite of the right being on your side."

And whilst I toyed with her charming daughter, she sent for a barrister. After hearing my case the counsel told me that my best way would be to tell the whole story to the sovereign as soon as possible.

"They took you to the house of ill-fame; they poured out the drugged wine which deprived you of your reason; they made you play in spite of their prince's prohibition (for gaming is strictly forbidden); in this company you were robbed of your jewels after they had made you lose an enormous sum. It's a hanging matter, and the duke's interest will be to do you justice, for an act of scoundrelism like this committed by his officers would dishonour him all over Europe."

I felt some repugnance to this course, for though the duke was a shameless libertine I did not like telling him such a disgraceful story. However, the case was a serious one, and after giving it due reflection I determined to wait on the dike on the following morning.

"As the duke gives audience to the first comer," I said to myself, "why should I not have as good a reception as a labouring man?" In this way I concluded that it would be no use to write to him, and I was on my way to the Court, when, at about twenty paces from the gate of the castle, I met my three gentlemen who accosted me rudely and said I had better make up my mind to pay, or else they would play the devil with me.

I was going on without paying any attention to them, when I felt myself rudely seized by the right arm. A natural impulse of self-defence made me put my hand to my sword, and I drew it in a manner that shewed I was in earnest. The officer of the guard came running up, and I complained that the three were assaulting me and endeavouring to hinder my approach to the prince. On enquiry being made, the sentry and the numerous persons who were present declared that I had only drawn in self-defence, so the officer decided that I had perfect liberty to enter the castle.

I was allowed to penetrate to the last antechamber without any obstacle being raised. Here I addressed myself to the chamberlain, demanding an audience with the sovereign, and he assured me that I should be introduced into the presence. But directly afterwards the impudent scoundrel who had taken hold of my arm came up and began to speak to the chamberlain in German. He said his say without my being able to contradict him, and his representations were doubtless not in my favour. Very possibly, too, the chamberlain was one of the gang, and I went from Herod to Pilate. An hour went by without my being able to see the prince, and then the chamberlain, who had assured me that I should have an audience, came and told me that I might go home, as the duke had heard all the circumstances of the case, and would no doubt see that justice was done me.

I saw at once that I should get no justice at all, and as I was walking away I thought how best I could get out of the difficulty. On my way I met Binetti, who knew how I was placed, and he asked me to come and dine with him, assuring me that the Austrian ambassador would take me under his protection, and that he would save me from the violent measures which the rascals no doubt intended to take, in spite of the chamberlain's assurances. I accepted the invitation, and Binetti's charming wife, taking the affair to heart, did not lose a moment in informing her lover, the ambassador, of all the circumstances.

This diplomatist came into the room with her, and after hearing all the details from my lips he said that in all probability the duke knew nothing about it.

"Write a brief account of the business," said he, "and I will lay it before the sovereign, who will no doubt see justice done."

I went to Binetti's desk, and as soon as I had written down my true relation I gave it, unsealed, to the ambassador, who assured me that it should be in the duke's hands in the course of an hour.

At dinner my country-woman assured me again that her lover should protect me, and we spent the day pleasantly enough; but towards evening my Spaniard came and assured me that if I returned to the inn I should be arrested, "for," said he, "an officer came to see you, and finding you were out he took up his position at the street door and has two soldiers standing at the foot of the staircase."

The Binetti said, "You must not go to the inn; stay here, where you have nothing to fear. Send for what you want, and we will wait and see what happens." I then gave orders to my Spaniard to go and fetch the belongings which were absolutely necessary to me.

At midnight the ambassador came in; we were still up, and he seemed pleased that his mistress had sheltered me. He assured me that my plea had been laid before the sovereign, but during the three days I was in the house I heard no more about it.

On the fourth day, whilst I was pondering as to how I should act, the ambassador received a letter from a minister requesting him, on behalf of the sovereign, to dismiss me from his house, as I had a suit pending with certain officers of his highness, and whilst I was with the ambassador justice could not take its course. The ambassador gave me the letter, and I saw that the minister promised that strict justice should be done me. There was no help for it; I had to make up my mind to return to my inn, but the

---

Binetti was so enraged that she began to scold her lover, at which he laughed, saying, with perfect truth, that he could not keep me there in defiance of the prince.

I re-entered the inn without meeting anyone, but when I had had my dinner and was just going to see my counsel an officer served me with a summons, which was interpreted to me by my landlord, which ordered me to appear forthwith before the notary appointed to take my deposition. I went to him with the officer of the court, and spent two hours with the notary, who wrote down my deposition in German while I gave it in Latin. When it was done he told me to sign my name; to which I answered that I must decline to sign a document I did not understand. He insisted on my doing it, but I was immovable. He then got in a rage and said I ought to be ashamed of myself for suspecting a notary's honour. I replied calmly that I had no doubts as to his honour, but that I acted from principle, and that as I did not understand what he had written I refused to sign it. I left him, and was accompanied by the officer to my own counsel, who said I had done quite right, and promised to call on me the next day to receive my power of attorney.

"And when I have done that," he said, "your business will be mine."

I was comforted by this man, who inspired me with confidence, and went back to the hotel, where I made a good supper and went tranquilly to sleep. Next morning, however, when I awoke, my Spaniard announced an officer who had followed him, and told me in good French that I must not be astonished to find myself a prisoner in my room, for being a stranger and engaged in a suit at law it was only right that the opposite party should be assured that I would not escape before judgment was given. He asked very politely for my sword, and to my great regret I was compelled to give it him. The hilt was of steel, exquisitely chased; it was a present from Madame d'Urfe, and was worth at least fifty louis.

I wrote a note to my counsel to tell him what had happened; he came to see me and assured me that I should only be under arrest for a few days.

As I was obliged to keep my room, I let my friends know of my confinement, and I received visits from dancers and ballet-girls, who were the only decent people I was acquainted with in that wretched Stuttgart, where I had better never have set foot. My situation was not pleasant to contemplate: I had been drugged, cheated, robbed, abused, imprisoned, threatened with a mulct of a hundred thousand francs, which would have stripped me to my shirt, as nobody knew the contents of my pocket-book. I could think of nothing else. I had written to Madame the Gardella, but to no purpose, as I got no answer. All the consolation I got was from Binetti, Toscani, and Baletti, who dined or supped with me every day. The three rascals came to see me one by one, and each tried to get me to give him money unknown to the other two, and each promised that if I would do that, he would get me out of the difficulty. Each would have been content with three or four hundred louis, but even if I had given that sum to one of them I had no guarantee that the others would desist from their persecution. Indeed, if I had done so I should have given some ground to their pretensions, and bad would have been made worse.

My answer was that they wearied me, and that I should be glad if they would desist from visiting me.

On the fifth day of my arrest the duke left for Frankfort; and the same day Binetti came and told me from her lover that the duke had promised the officers not to interfere, and that I was therefore in danger of an iniquitous sentence. His advice was to neglect no means of getting out of the difficulty, to sacrifice all my property, diamonds, and jewellery, and thus to obtain a release from my enemies. The Binetti, like a wise woman, disliked this counsel, and I relished it still less, but she had to perform her commission.

I had jewellery and lace to the value of more than a hundred thousand francs, but I could not resolve to make the sacrifice. I did not know which way to turn or where to go, and while I was in this state of mind my barrister came in. He spoke as follows:

"Sir, all my endeavors on your behalf have been unsuccessful. There is a party against you which seems to have support in some high quarter, and which silences the voice of justice. It is my duty to warn you that unless you find some way of arranging matters with these rascals you are a ruined man. The judgment given by the police magistrate, a rascal like the rest of them, is of a summary character, for as a stranger you will not be allowed to have recourse to the delays of the law. You would require bail to do that. They have managed to procure witnesses who swear that you are a professional gamester, that it was you who seduced the three officers into the house of your countryman Peccini, that it is not true that your wine was drugged that you did not lose your watches nor your snuff-box, for, they say, these articles will be found in your mails when your goods are sold. For that you will only have to wait till to-morrow or the day after, and do not think that I am deceiving you in any particular, or you will be sorry for it. They will come here and empty your mails, boxes, and pockets, a list will be made, and they will be sold by auction the same day. If the sum realized is greater than the debt the surplus will go in costs, and you may depend upon it that a very small sum will be returned to you; but if, on the other hand, the sum is not sufficient to pay everything, including the debt, costs, expenses of the auction, etc., you will be enrolled as a common soldier in the forces of His Most Serene Highness. I heard it said to the officer, who is your greatest creditor, that the four Louis enlistment money would be taken into account, and that the duke would be glad to get hold of such a fine man."

The barrister left me without my noticing him. I was so petrified by what he had said. I was in such a state of collapse that in less than an hour all the liquids in my body must have escaped. I, a common soldier in the army of a petty sovereign like the duke, who only existed by the horrible traffic in human flesh which he carried on after the manner of the Elector of Hesse. I, despoiled by those knaves, the victim of an iniquitous sentence. Never! I would endeavour to hit upon some plan to gain time.

I began by writing to my chief creditor that I had decided to come to an agreement with them, but I wished them all to wait upon my notary, with witnesses, to put a formal close to the action and render me a free man again.

I calculated that one of them was sure to be on duty on the morrow, and thus I should gain a day at any rate. In the mean time I hoped to discover some way of escape.

I next wrote to the head of the police, whom I styled "your excellency" and "my lord," begging him to vouchsafe his all-powerful protection. I told him that I had resolved on selling all my property to put an end to the suit which threatened to overwhelm me, and I begged him to suspend the proceedings, the cost of which could only add to my difficulties. I also asked him to send me a trustworthy man to value my effects as soon as I had come to an agreement with my creditors, with whom I begged for his good offices. When I had done I sent my Spaniard to deliver the letters.

The officer to whom I had written, who pretended that I was his debtor to the amount of two thousand Louis, came to see me after dinner. I was in bed; and I told him I thought I had fever. He began to offer his sympathy, and, genuine or not, I was pleased with it. He told me he had just had some conversation with the chief of the police, who had shewn him my letter.

"You are very wise," said he, "in consenting to a composition, but we need not all three be present. I have full powers from the other two, and that will be sufficient for the notary."

"I am in bad enough case," I replied, "for you to grant me the favour of seeing you all together; I cannot think you will refuse me."

"Well, well, you shall be satisfied, but if you are in a hurry to leave Stuttgart I must warn you that we cannot come before Monday, for we are on duty for the next four days."

"I am sorry to hear it, but I will wait. Give me your word of honour that all proceedings shall be suspended in the mean time."

"Certainly; here is my hand, and you may reckon on me. In my turn I have a favour to ask. I like your post-chaise; will you let me have it for what it cost you?"

"With pleasure."

"Be kind enough to call the landlord, and tell him in my presence that the carriage belongs to me."

I had the landlord upstairs and did as the rascal had asked me, but mine host told him that he could dispose of it after he had paid for it, and with that he turned his back on him and left the room.

"I am certain of having the chaise," said the officer, laughing. He then embraced me, and went away

I had derived so much pleasure from my talk with him that I felt quite another man. I had four days before me; it was a rare piece of good luck.

Some hours after, an honest-looking fellow who spoke Italian well came to tell me, from the chief of police, that my creditors would meet on the ensuing Monday, and that he himself was appointed to value my goods. He advised me to make it a condition of the agreement that my goods should not be sold by auction, and that my creditors should consider his valuation as final and binding. He told me that I should congratulate myself if I followed his advice.

I told him that I would not forget his services, and begged him to examine my mails and my jewel-box. He examined everything and told me that my lace alone was worth twenty thousand francs. "In all," he added, "your goods are worth more than a hundred thousand francs, but I promise to tell your adversaries another story, Thus, if you can persuade them to take half their debt, you will get off with half your effects."

"In that ease," I said, "you shall have fifty louis, and here are six as an earnest."

"I am grateful to you, and you can count upon my devotion. The whole town and the duke as well know your creditors to be knaves, but they have their reasons for refusing to see their conduct in its true light."

I breathed again, and now all my thoughts were concentrated on making my escape with all I possessed, my poor chaise excepted. I had a difficult task before me, but not so difficult a one as my flight from The Leads, and the recollection of my great escape gave me fresh courage.

My first step was to ask Toscani, Baletti, and the dancer Binetti to supper, as I had measures to concert with these friends of mine, whom I could rely on, and who had nothing to fear from the resentment of three rascals.

After we had had a good supper I told them how the affair stood, and that I was determined to escape, and to carry my goods with me. "And now," I said, "I want your advice."

After a brief silence Binetti said if I could get to his house I could lower myself down from a window, and once on the ground I should be outside the town walls and at a distance of a hundred paces from the high road, by which I could travel post and be out of the duke's dominions by daybreak. Thereupon Baletti opened the window and found that it would be impossible to escape that way, on account of a wooden roof above a shop. I looked out also, and seeing that he was right I said that I should no doubt hit on some way of making my escape from the inn, but what troubled me chiefly was my luggage. The Toscani then said:—

"You will have to abandon your mails, which you could not take off without attracting attention, and you must send all your effects to my house. I engage to deliver safely whatever you may put in my care. I will take away your effects under my clothes in several journeys, and I can begin to-night."

Baletti thought this idea a good one, and said that to do it the quicker his wife would come and help. We fixed on this plan, and I promised Binetti to be with him at midnight on Sunday, even if I had to stab the sentry, who was at my door all day, but who went away at night after locking me in. Baletti said he would provide me with a faithful servant, and a post-chaise with swift horses, which would take my effects in other mails. To make the best use of the time, the Toscani began to load herself, putting two of my suits of clothes under her dress. For the next few days my friends served me so well that, at midnight on Saturday, my mails and my dressing case were empty; I kept back all the jewellery intending to carry it in my pocket.

On Sunday, the Toscani brought me the keys of the two mails, in which she had put my goods; and Baletti came also to tell me that all the necessary measures had been taken, and that I should find a post-chaise, under the charge of his servant, waiting for me on the high road. So far good, and the reader shall now hear how I contrived to escape from my inn.

The sentry confined himself to a small ante-chamber, where he walked up and down, without ever coming into my room, except at my invitation. As soon as he heard that I had gone to bed he locked the door, and went off till the next day. He used to sup on a little table in a corner of the ante-room; his food being sent out by me. Profiting by my knowledge of his habits, I gave my Spaniard the following instructions:

"After supper, instead of going to bed, I shall hold myself in readiness for leaving my room, and I shall leave it when I see the light extinguished in the ante-room, while I shall take care that my candle be so placed as not to shew any light outside, or to reflect my shadow. Once out of my room, I shall have no difficulty in reaching the stairs, and my escape will be accomplished. I shall go to Binetti's, leave the town by his house, and wait for you at Furstenburg. No one can hinder you from joining me in the course of a day or two. So when you see me ready in my room, and this will be whilst the sentry is having his supper, put out the candle on the table: you can easily manage to do so whilst snuffing it. You will then take it to re-light it, and I shall seize that moment to get off in the darkness. When you conclude that I have got out of the ante-room, you can come back to the soldier with the lighted candle, and you can help him to finish his bottle. By that time I shall be safe, and when you tell him I have gone to bed he will come to the door, wish me good night, and after locking the door and putting the key in his pocket he will go away with you. It is not likely that he will come in and speak to me when he hears I have gone to bed."

Nevertheless, as he might possibly take it into his head to come into the room, I carefully arranged a wig-block in a night-cap on the pillow, and huddled up the coverlet so as to deceive a casual glance.

All my plans were successful, as I heard afterwards from my Spaniard. Whilst he was drinking with the sentry I was getting on my great coat, girding on my hanger (I had no longer a sword), and putting my loaded pistols in my pocket. As soon as the darkness told me that Le Duc had put out the candle I went out softly, and reached the staircase without making the least noise. Once there the rest was easy, for the stair led into the passage, and the passage to the main door, which was always open till nearly midnight.

I stepped out along the street, and at a quarter to twelve I got to Binetti's, and found his wife looking out for me at the window. When I was in the room, whence I intended to escape, we lost no time. I threw my overcoat to Baletti, who was standing in the ditch below, up to the knees in mud, and binding a strong cord round my waist I embraced the Binetti and Baletti's wife, who lowered me down as gently as possible. Baletti received me in his arms, I cut the cord, and after taking my great coat I followed his footsteps. We strode through the mud, and going along a hedge we reached the high road in a state of exhaustion, although it was not more than a hundred paces as the crow flies from where we stood to the house. At a little distance off, beside a small wayside inn, we found the postchaise in which sat Baletti's servant. He got out, telling us that the postillion had just gone into the inn to have a glass of beer and light his pipe. I took the good servant's place, and gave him a reward, and begged them both to be gone, saying I would manage all the rest myself.

It was April and, 1760—my birthday—and a remarkable period in my career, although my whole life has been filled with adventures, good or bad.

I had been in the carriage for two or three minutes when the postillion came and asked me if we had much longer to wait. He thought he was speaking to the same person that he had left in the chaise, and I did not undeceive him. "Drive on," I answered, "and make one stage of it from here to Tubingen, without changing horses at Waldenbach." He followed my instructions, and we went along at a good pace, but I had a strong inclination to laugh at the face he made when he saw me at Tubingen. Baletti's servant was a youth, and slightly built; I was tall, and quite a man. He opened his eyes to their utmost width, and told me I was not the same gentleman that was in the carriage when he started. "You're drunk," said I, putting in his hand four times what he was accustomed to get, and the poor devil did not say a word. Who has not experienced the persuasive influence of money? I went on my journey, and did not stop till I reached Furstenburg, where I was quite safe.

I had eaten nothing on the way, and by the time I got to the inn I was dying of hunger. I had a good supper brought to me, and then I went to bed and slept well. As soon as I awoke I wrote to my three rascals. I promised to wait ten days for them at the place from which I dated the letter, and I challenged them to a duel a l'outrance, swearing that I would publish their cowardice all over Europe if they refused to measure swords with me. I next wrote to the Toscani, to Baletti, and to the good-natured mistress of the Austrian ambassador, commending Le Duc to their care, and thanking them for their friendly help.

The three rascals did not come, but the landlord's two daughters, both of them pretty, made me pass the three days very agreeably.

On the fourth day, towards noon, I had the pleasure of seeing my faithful Spaniard riding into the town carrying his portmanteau on his saddle

"Sir," said he, "all Stuttgart knows you to be here, and I fear, lest the three officers who were too cowardly to accept your challenge may have you assassinated. If you are wise you will set out for Switzerland forthwith."

"That's cowardly, my lad," said I. "Don't be afraid about me, but tell me all that happened after my escape."

"As soon as you were gone, sir, I carried out your instructions, and helped the poor devil of a sentry to empty his bottle, though he would have willingly dispensed with my assistance in the matter; I then told him you had gone to bed, and he locked the door as usual, and went away after shaking me by the hand. After he had gone I went to bed. Next morning the worthy man was at his post by nine o'clock, and at ten the three officers came, and on my telling them that you were still asleep they went away, bidding me come to a coffee-house, and summon them when you got up. As they waited and waited to no purpose, they came again at noon, and told the soldier to open the door. What followed amused me, though I was in some danger in the midst of the rascals.

"They went in, and taking the wig-block for your head they came up to the bed and politely wished you good morning. You took no notice, so one of them proceeded to give you a gentle shake, and the bauble fell and rolled along the floor. I roared with laughter at the sight of their amazement.

"'You laugh, do you, rascal? Tell us where your master is.' And to give emphasis to their words they accompanied them with some strokes of the cane.

"I was not going to stand this sort of thing, so I told them, with an oath, that if they did not stop I should defend myself, adding that I was not my master's keeper, and advising them to ask the sentry.

"The sentry on his part swore by all the saints that you must have escaped by the window, but in spite of this a corporal was summoned, and the poor man was sent to prison.

"The clamour that was going on brought up the landlord, who opened your mails, and on finding them empty said that he would be well enough paid by your postchaise, replying only with a grin to the officer who pretended you had given it him.

"In the midst of the tumult a superior officer came up, who decided that you must have escaped through the window, and ordered the sentry to be set at liberty on the spot. Then came my turn, for, as I kept on laughing and answered all questions by 'I don't know,' these gentleman had me taken to prison, telling me I should stay there till I informed them where you, or at least your effects, could be found.

"The next day one of them came to the prison, and told me that unless I confessed I should undoubtedly be sent to the galleys.

"'On the faith of a Spaniard,' I answered, 'I know nothing, but if I did it would be all the same to you, for no one can make an honest servant betray his master.'

"At this the rascal told the turnkey to give me a taste of the lash, and after this had been done I was set at liberty.

"My back was somewhat scarified, but I had the proud consciousness of having done my duty, and I went back and slept at the inn, where they were glad to see me. Next morning everyone knew you were here and had sent a challenge to the three sharpers, but the universal opinion was that they were too knowing to risk their lives by meeting you. Nevertheless, Madame Baletti told me to beg you to leave Furstenburg, as they might very likely have you assassinated. The landlord sold your chaise and your mails to the Austrian ambassador, who, they say, let you escape from a window in the apartment occupied by his mistress. No one offered to prevent me coming here.

"Three hours after Le Duc's arrival I took post and went to Schaffhaus, and from there to Zurich, with hired horses, as there are no posts in Switzerland. At Zurich I put up at the 'Sward,' an excellent inn.

"After supper, powdering over my arrival in Zurich where I had dropped from the clouds as it were, I began, to reflect seriously upon my present situation and the events of my past life. I recalled my misfortunes and scrutinized my conduct; and was not long in concluding that all I had suffered was through my own fault, and that when fortune would have crowned me with happiness I had persistently trifled that happiness away. I had just succeeded in escaping from a trap where I might have perished, or at least have been overwhelmed with shame, and I shuddered at the thought. I resolved to be no more fortune's plaything, but to escape entirely from her hands. I calculated my assets and found I was possessed of a hundred thousand crowns. 'With that,' said I, 'I can live secure amidst the changes and chances of this life, and I shall at last experience true happiness.'"

I went to bed pondering over these fancies, and my sleep was full of happy dreams. I saw myself dwelling in a retired spot amidst peace and plenty. I thought I was surrounded on all sides by a fair expanse of country which belonged to me, where I enjoyed that freedom the world cannot give. My dreams had all the force of reality, till a sudden awakening at day-break came to give them the lie. But the imaginary bliss I had enjoyed had so taken my fancy that I could not rest till I realized it. I arose, dressed myself hastily, and went out, fasting, without knowing where I was going.

I walked on and on, absorbed in contemplation, and did not really awake till I found myself in a ravine between two lofty mountains. Stepping forward I reached a valley surrounded by mountains on all sides, and in the distance a fine church, attached to a pile of buildings, magnificently situated. I guessed it to be a monastery, and I made my way towards it.

The church door was open, and I went in and was amazed at the rich marbles and the beauty of the altars; and, after hearing the last mass, I went to the sacristy and found myself in a crowd of Benedictines.

The abbot, whom I recognized by his cross, came towards me and asked if I wished to see the church and monastery. I replied that I should be delighted, and he, with two other brethren, offered to shew me all. I saw their rich ornaments, chasubles embroidered with gold and pearls, the sacred vessels adorned with diamonds and other precious stones, a rich balustrade, etc.

As I understood German very imperfectly and the Swiss dialect (which is hard to acquire and bears the same relation to German that Genoese has to Italian) not at all, I began to speak Latin, and asked the abbot if the church had been built for long. Thereupon the very reverend father entered into a long history, which would have made me repent my inquisitiveness if he had not finished by saying that the church was consecrated by Jesus Christ Himself. This was carrying its foundation rather far back, and no doubt my face expressed some surprise, for to convince me of the truth of the story the abbot bade me follow him into the church, and there on a piece of marble pavement he shewed me the imprint of the foot of Jesus, which He had left there at the moment of the consecration, to convince the infidels and to save the bishop the trouble of consecrating the church.

The abbot had had this divinely revealed to him in a dream, and going into the church to verify the vision he saw the print of the Divine Foot, and gave thanks to the Lord.

The End